Giovanni Pico della Mirandola:

His life by his nephew Giovanni Francesco Pico, also three of his letters, his Interpretation of Psalm XVI; his Twelve rules of a Christian and his Deprecatory hymn to God

by
Giovanni Francesco Pico

translated by
Sir Thomas More

INTRODUCTION.

GIOVANNI PICO DELLA MIRAN-
DOLA, "the Phœnix of the wits," is
one of those writers whose personality
will always count for a great deal more
than their works.   His extreme, almost
feminine beauty, high rank, and chival-
rous character, his immense energy and versatility, his
insatiable thirst for knowledge, his passion for theorizing,
his rare combination of intellectual hardihood with genuine
devoutness of spirit, his extraordinary precocity, and his
premature death, make up a personality so engaging that
his name at any rate, and the record of his brief life,
must always excite the interest and enlist the sympathy
of mankind, though none but those, few in any genera-
tion, who love to loiter curiously in the bypaths of literature and philosophy, will ever care to follow his eager
spirit through the labyrinths of recondite speculation
which it once thridded with such high and generous hope.

For us, indeed, of the latter end of the nineteenth
century, trained in the exact methods, guided by the
steady light of modern philosophy and criticism, it is no
easy matter to enter sympathetically into the thoughts of

men who lived while as yet these were not, men who
spent their strength in errant efforts, in blind gropings in
the dark, on abortive half-solutions or no-solutions of
problems too difficult for them, mere *ignes fatui*, it would
seem, or at best mere brilliant meteor stars illuminating
the intellectual firmament with a transitory trail of light,
and then vanishing to leave the darkness more visible, yet
without whose mistakes and failures and apparently futile
waste of power philosophy and criticism would not have
come into being.

Among such wandering meteoric apparitions not the
least brilliant was Pico della Mirandola. Born in 1463,
he grew to manhood in time to witness and participate in
the effectual revival of Greek learning in Italy ; yet his
earliest bias was scholastic, and a schoolman in grain he
remained to the day of his death. How strongly he had
felt the influence of the schoolmen, how little disposed he
was to follow the humanistic hue and cry of indiscriminate
condemnation, may be judged from the eloquent apology
for them which, in the shape of a letter to his friend
Ermolao Barbaro, he published in 1485. It was the
fashion to stigmatize the schoolmen as barbarians because
they knew no Greek and could not write classical Latin.
That was the head and front of their offending in the eyes of
men who had no idea of a better method of philosophizing
than theirs, nor indeed any interest in philosophy, mere
rhetoricians, grammarians, and pedagogues, while at any
rate the schoolmen, however rude their style, were serious
thinkers, who in grappling with the deepest problems of
science human and divine displayed the rarest patience,
sagacity, subtlety and ingenuity. Such is the gist of Pico's
plea on behalf of the " barbarians," in urging which he
exhausts the resources of rhetoric, and the ingenuity of

the advocate; nor is there reason to doubt that it represents at least the embers of a very genuine enthusiasm. That challenge, also, which he issued at Rome, and in every university in Italy in the winter of 1486-7, summoning as if by clarion call every intellectual knight-errant in the peninsula to try conclusions with him in public disputation in the eternal city after the feast of Epiphany, does it not recall the celebrated exploit of Duns Scotus at Paris, when, according to the tradition, he won the title of Doctor Subtilis by refuting two hundred objections to the doctrine of the Immaculate Conception of the Virgin Mary in a single day?   Only, as befitted " a great lord of Italy," Pico's tournament is to be on a grander scale. Duns had but one thesis to defend; Pico offers to maintain nine hundred, and lest poverty should reduce the number of his antagonists he offers to pay their travelling expenses.   Moreover, to Duns, Aquinas, and other of the schoolmen, Pico is beholden for not a few of his theses; of the rest, some are drawn direct from Plato, others from Neo-Pythagorean, Neo-Platonic and syncretist writers, while a certain number appear to be original. Pico, however, was not so fortunate as Duns: the church smelt heresy in his propositions, and Pope Innocent VIII., though he had at first authorised, was induced to prohibit their discussion. (Bull dated 4th August, 1487). Thirteen were selected for examination by a special commission and were pronounced heretical. Pico, however, so far from bowing to its decision, wrote in hot haste an elaborate "Apologia" or defence of his orthodoxy, which, had it not been more ingenious than conclusive, might perhaps have been accepted; as it was, it only brought him into further trouble.

This Apology "elucubrated," as he tells, "properante

stilo" in twenty nights, Pico dedicated to Lorenzo de'
Medici, modestly describing it as "exiguum sane munus,
sed fidei meae, sed observantiae profecto in omne tempus
erga te maxime non leve testimonium," "a trifling gift
indeed, but as far as possible from being a slight token
of my loyalty, nay, of my devotion to you." Hasty
though its composition was, it certainly displays no lack
of either ingenuity, subtlety, acuteness, learning, or style.
Evidently written out of a full mind, it represents Pico's
mature judgment upon the abstruse topics which it
handles, and is a veritable masterpiece of scholastic argu-
mentation. After a brief prologue detailing the circum-
stances which gave occasion to the work Pico proceeds to
discuss *seriatim* the thirteen "damnatæ conclusiones,"
and the several objections which had been made to them.
The tone throughout is severe and dry and singularly
free from heat or asperity. Some of the theses are treated
at considerable length, others dismissed in a page or two,
or even less. Altogether, when the rapidity of its composition is borne in mind, the treatise appears little less a
prodigy.

The obnoxious theses were as follows :—(1) That
Christ did not truly and in real presence, but only *quoad
effectum*, descend into hell; (2) that a mortal sin of
finite duration is not deserving of eternal but only of
temporal punishment; (3) that neither the cross of
Christ, nor any image, ought to be adored in the way of
worship; (4) that God cannot assume a nature of any
kind whatsoever, but only a rational nature; (5) that no
science affords a better assurance of the divinity of Christ
than magical and cabalistic science; (6) that assuming
the truth of the ordinary doctrine that God can take upon
himself the nature of any creature whatsoever, it is pos-

sible for the body of Christ to be present on the altar without the conversion of the substance of the bread or the annihilation of "paneity;" (7) that it is more rational to believe that Origen is saved than that he is damned; (8) that as no one's opinions are just such as he wills them to be, so no one's beliefs are just such as he wills them to be; (9) that the inseparability of subject and accident may be maintained consistently with the doctrine of transubstantiation; (10) that the words "hoc est corpus" pronounced during the consecration of the bread are to be taken "materialiter" (i.e., as a mere recital) and not "significative" (i.e., as denoting an actual fact); (11) that the miracles of Christ are a most certain proof of his divinity, by reason not of the works themselves, but of his manner of doing them; (12) that it is more improper to say of God that he is intelligent, or intellect, than of an angel that it is a rational soul; (13) that the soul knows nothing in act and distinctly but itself.

It is undeniable that some of these propositions smack somewhat rankly of heresy, and Pico's ingenuity is taxed to the uttermost to give them even a semblance of congruity with the doctrines of the Church. The following, however, is the gist of his defence. Christ, he argues, did actually descend into hell, but only in spirit, not in bodily presence; eternal punishment is inflicted on the finally impenitent sinner not for his sins done in the flesh, which are finite, but for his impenitence, which is necessarily infinite; the cross is to be adored, but only as a symbol, not in and for itself, for which he cites Scotus, admitting that St. Thomas is against him. The thesis that God cannot take upon himself a nature of any kind whatsoever, but only a rational nature, must be understood without prejudice to the omnipotence of God, which is not in question ; God cannot assume the nature of any irrational creature, because by the very act of so doing he necessarily raises it to himself, endows it with a rational nature. The thesis that no science gives us better assurance of the divinity of Christ than magical and cabalistic science referred to such sciences only as do not rest on revelation, and among them to the science of natural magic, which treats of the virtues and activities of natural agents and their relations *inter se*, and that branch only of cabalistic science which is concerned with the virtues of celestial bodies ; which of all natural sciences furnish the most convincing proof of the divinity of Christ, because they show that his miracles could not have been performed by natural agencies. The sixth thesis must not be understood as if Pico maintained that the bread was not converted into the body of Christ, but only that it is possible that the bread and the body may be mysteriously linked together without the one being converted into the other, which would be quite consistent with the words of St. Paul, 1 Cor. x. 16: "The bread which we break is it not the communion of the body of Christ ? " if interpreted figuratively. With regard to the salvation of Origen, Pico plunges with evident zest into the old controversy as to the authenticity of the heretical passages in that writer's works, and urges that his damnation can at most be no more than a pious opinion. In justification of the position that belief is not a mere matter of will he cites the authority of Aristotle and St. Augustine, adding a brief summary of the evidences of the Christian faith, to wit, prophecy, the harmony of the Scriptures, the authority of their authors, the reasonableness of their contents, the unreasonableness of their contents, the unreasonableness of particular heresies, the stability of the Church, the miracles. As to transubstantiation, Pico professes himself to hold the doctrine of the Church, merely adding thereto the pious opinion that the Thomist distinction between real existence and essence is consistent with the theory that the bread itself remains in spite of the transmutation of its substance, and thus with the doctrine of the inseparability of subject and accident ; as for the words " hoc est corpus," it appears from their context and their place in the office that they are not to be taken literally, for the priest, when in consecrating the bread he says, " Take, eat," does not suit the action to the word by offering the bread to the communicants, but takes it himself, and so when in consecrating the wine he says, "qui pro vobis et pro multis effundetur," it is not to be supposed, as if the words were to be taken literally it must be supposed, that he means that the blood of Christ actually will be shed, or that he does not mean to claim the benefit of it for himself as well as the congregation, and the "many." That the value of Christ's miracles as evidences of his divinity lies rather in the way in which they were wrought than in the works themselves, is supported by Christ's own words in St. John xiv. 12 : " Verily, verily, I say unto you, He that believeth on me, the works that I do shall he do also ; and greater works than these shall he do ; because I go to my Father ;" which are quite inconsistent with the idea that the works are themselves evidence of his divinity. In support of the proposition that intellect or intelligence cannot properly be ascribed to God, Pico invokes the authority of Dionysius the Areopagite, who holds the same doctrine, but does not on that account deny to God an altogether superior faculty of cognition, even farther removed from angelic intelligence than that is from human reason. The last proposition, viz., that the soul knows nothing in act and distinctly but itself, being extremely subtle and profound, Pico forbears to enlarge upon it, pointing out, however, that it has the authority of St. Augustine in its favour. The reference is to the De Trinitate, x. 14.[1] The doctrine itself is of peculiar interest, for in it lay the germ of the Cartesian philosophy.

Pico concludes the "Apologia" with an eloquent appeal to his critics to judge him fairly, which was so little heeded that some of them saw fit to impugn its good faith, and raised such a clamour about it that Pico, who in the meantime had gone to France, was peremptorily recalled to Rome by the Pope. He complied, but through the influence of Lorenzo was permitted to reside in the Benedictine monastery at Fiesole, while the new charge was under investigation. Meanwhile Garsias, Bishop of Ussel, published (1489) an elaborate examination of the " Apologia," nor did Pico hear the last of the affair until shortly before his death, when Alexander VI., by a Bull dated 18th June, 1493, acquitted him of heresy and assured him of immunity from further annoyance.

An oration on man and his place in nature—with which Pico had designed to introduce his theses to the

[1] Utrum emin aeris sit vis vivendi, reminiscendi, volendi, cogitandi, sciendi, judicandi; an ignis, an cerebri, an sanguinis, an atomorum, an præter usitata quatuor elementa quinti nescio cujus corporis, an ipsius carnis nostræ compago vel temperamentum hæc efficere valeat, dubitaverunt homines : et alius hoc, alius aliud affirmare conatus est. Vivere se tamen et meminisse, et intelligere, et velle, et cogitare, et scire, et judicare quis dubitet? Quandoquidem etiam si dubitat, vivit : si dubitat unde dubitet, meminit; si dubitat, dubitare se intelligit; si dubitat, certus esse vult; si dubitat, cogitat; si dubitat, scit se nescire; si dubitat, judicat non se temere consentire oportere. Quisquis igitur aliunde dubitat, de his omnibus dubitare non debet : quæ si non essent de ulla re dubitare non posset.

learned audience which he had hoped to gather about him to listen to the discussion—was not published until after his death. The theme is the familiar one of the dignity of man as the only terrestrial creature endowed with free will, and thus capable of developing into an angel and even becoming one with God, or declining into a brute or even a vegetable. On this Pico descants at some length and with much eloquence, and a great display of erudition—Schoolman and Neo-Platonist, Cabalist and Pythagorean, Moses and Plato, Job, Seneca, Cicero, and the Peripatetics jostling one another in his pages in the most *bizarre* fashion. With Pico, as with Dante, theology is the queen of the sciences, and the true end of man is so to purify the soul by the practice of virtue and the study of philosophy—moral and natural—as that it may be capable of the knowledge and the love of God. His own theological speculations are contained in three works, viz.: (1) a commentary on the first twenty-six verses of the first chapter of Genesis, published in 1489, under the title of "Heptaplus," and dedicated to Lorenzo de' Medici; (2) an essay towards the reconcilation of Plato and Aristotle, entitled "De Ente et Uno," published in 1491; (3) a commentary on Girolamo Benivieni's "Canzone dello Amore Celeste e Divino," the date of which has not been precisely fixed.

This curious trilogy is a signal example of the insane extravagances into which an acute and subtle intellect may be led by philosophical and theological *arrière pensée*. Pico's problem is essentially the same with that on which the most powerful and ingenious minds of the Middle Ages had spent their strength in vain, to wit— how to reconcile theology and philosophy. The difference is that, whereas the older thinkers had but little knowledge of any other philosopher than Aristotle, and knew him but imperfectly, Pico in the full tide of the renaissance has to grapple with the gigantic task of reconciling Catholic doctrine not merely with Aristotle, but with Plato, the Neo-Platonists, Neo-Pythagoreans, the pseudo-Dionysius the Areopagite, the Orphic and Hermetic theosophies, and indeed with whatever of recondite, obscure, and mysterious in that kind the Pagan world had given birth to. The result is what might be expected — the wildest possible jumble of incompatible ideas, which not even the most dexterous legerdemain can twist into the remotest semblance of congruity.

In the dedicatory letter prefixed to the " Heptaplus " Pico explains to Lorenzo the scheme of the work, and the motives which induced him to undertake it. Besides the inestimable advantage which he derived from being the immediate recipient of divine revelation, Moses, it appears, was the greatest of all philosophers. Was he not versed in all the science of the Egyptians, and was not Egypt the source whence the Greeks drew their inspiration ? Was not Plato rightly called by Numenius[1] Μωσῆς Ἀττικίζων ? True it is that Moses has not the least of the appearance of a philosopher, but even in the account of the creation seems only to be telling a very plain and simple story, but that must not be allowed to detract from his claims. Doubtless he veiled a profound meaning under this superficial show of simplicity, and spoke in enigmas, or allegories, even as Plato and Jesus Christ were wont to do, in order that they might not be

[1] Numenius of Apameia in Syria, a syncretistic philosopher, supposed to have lived in the age of the Antonines. For the phrase see Mullach, *Frag. Phil. Græc.* iii. 167.

understood except by those to whom it was given to understand mysteries.

In all true wisdom there should be an element of mystery; it would not be right that everyone should be able to understand it. The task of interpreting the Mosaic account of the creation has been taken in hand by a host of writers, who have struggled mightily with three cardinal difficulties, which, it would seem, they have one and all failed to surmount. These difficulties are (1) to avoid attributing to Moses commonplace or inadequate ideas; (2) to make the interpretation consecutive and consistent from beginning to end; (3) to bring him into harmony with subsequent thinkers. Where his predecessors have failed Pico hopes to succeed.

The interpretation is worthy of the proem. In the threefold division of the Tabernacle Pico finds a type of the three spheres—angelic or intelligible, celestial, and sublunary—which, with man, the microcosm, make up the universe; and thus has no difficulty in understanding why the veil of the Temple was rent when Christ opened a way for man into the super-celestial sphere. These four worlds are all one, not only because all have the same first principle and the same final cause, and are linked together by certain general harmonies and affinities, but also because whatever is found in the sublunary sphere has its counterpart in the other two, but of a nobler character (*meliore nota*). Thus to terrestrial fire corresponds in the celestial sphere the sun; in the super-celestial, seraphic intelligence. Similarly, what is water on earth is in the heavens the moon, and in the super-celestial region cherubic intelligence. "The elementary fire burns, the celestial vivifies, the super-celestial loves." What cherubic intelligence does Pico forgets to say; but

fire and water being opposed, it is clear that it ought
to hate.

In the intelligible world God, surrounded by nine
orders of angels, unmoved Himself, draws all to Himself; to whom in the celestial world corresponds the
stable empyrean with its nine revolving spheres; in the
sublunary world the first matter with its three elementary
forms, earth, water, and fire, the three orders of vegetable
life, herbs, plants, and trees, and the three sorts of
" sensual souls," zoophytic, brutish, human, making together "nine spheres of corruptible forms."

Man, the microcosm, unites all three spheres; having
a body mixed of the elements, a vegetal soul, and the
senses of the brute, reason or spirit, which holds of the
celestial sphere, and an angelic intellect, in virtue of
which he is the very image of God.

Now it is true that Moses in his account of the creation
appears to ignore all this, but it is not for us on that account
to impute to him ignorance of it. On the contrary, we must
suppose that his cosmogony is equally true of each of the
four worlds which make up the universe, and must accordingly give it a fourfold interpretation. A fifth chapter will
be rendered necessary by the difference between the four
worlds, and a sixth by their affinities and community.

We have thus six chapters corresponding with the six
days of creation. A seventh is devoted to expounding the
meaning of the Sabbath rest; and to indicate this sevenfold
division of the work Pico entitles it " Heptaplus."

The plural method of interpreting Scripture, it must
be observed, was by no means peculiar to Pico, indeed
was in common use in his day. As a rule, however,
commentators were content with three senses, which they
distinguished as mystical, anagogical, and allegorical. To

Pico's philosophic mind this, no doubt, seemed a pitiful empiricism. For what was the ground of the triple method? Why these three senses and no more? He scorned such grovelling economy and rule of thumb, and determined to place the interpretation of the Mosaic cosmogony once for all on a firm and philosophic basis. Digging, accordingly, deep into the nature of things for the root, as he calls it, of his exegesis, he comes upon the Ptolemaic system with its central earth surrounded by its nine concentric revolving spheres, the nearest that of the moon, the most remote that of the fixed stars, in the interspace the solar and other planetary spheres, and beyond all the stable empyrean. To this he joins the Platonic theory of an intelligible world behind the phenomenal, and the Christian idea of heaven, borrows from the pseudo-Dionysius the Areopagite his nine orders of angels to correspond with the nine celestial spheres, discerns in the stable empyrean the type of the immutability of God, in matter as the promise and potency of all things, the evidence of His infinite power and fulness, throws in the Neo-Platonic doctrine of the microcosm and macrocosm, and lo! the work is done, and a cosmology constructed, which to elicit from Genesis may well demand a sevenfold method of interpretation. The minor details of this curious mosaic, to wit, the correspondence between the nine spheres of corruptible forms and the nine planets, between seraphic intelligence and the sun, between cherubic intelligence and the moon, seem, for what they are worth, to be all Pico's own.

Having thus found, as he thinks, a philosophic basis for his exegetical method, Pico proceeds to apply it to the Mosaic text with the utmost rigour and vigour. It would be tedious to follow him through all the minutiæ of his elaborate and extraordinary interpretation. A few examples of his art will amply suffice; and we cannot do better than begin at the beginning. What, then, did Moses mean by "In the beginning"? The solution of this weighty problem Pico plainly regards as his greatest triumph, and accordingly reserves it for the closing chapter, when he introduces it with a mighty flourish of trumpets. These pregnant words, "In the beginning," contain, it appears, the following mystic sentence: "Pater in Filio et per Filium, principium et finem, sive quietem, creavit caput, ignem, et fundamentum magni hominis fœdere bono," which is elicited from them by various dexterous permutations and combinations of the letters which make up their Hebrew equivalent. The key to the interpretation of the sentence is found in the idea of the microcosm.

Man being the microcosm, the macrocosm, or universe, may be called "magnus homo," whose "caput," or head, is the supercelestial or intelligible world, while his "ignis," fire, or heart, is the celestial world or empyrean, and his "fundamentum," or base, the sublunary sphere, all which are bound together "fœdere bono," by ties of kinship and congruity. In plain English, then, the initial words of the first chapter of Genesis mean, according to Pico :—"The Father in the Son, and by the Son, who is the beginning and the end, or rest, created the head, the heart, and the lower parts of the great man fitly joined together;" and thus contain an implicit prophecy of the Christian dispensation.

After this splendid *tour de force*, everything else in Pico's exposition will seem tame and trivial. We may observe, however, that four being a square number, he finds in the fourth day an adumbration of the fulness of time in which Christ came to earth; in the sun, moon, and stars types of

Christ, His Church, and His Apostles; in the waters under
the firmament, which on the third day were gathered together unto one place, a type of the Gentiles; in the
earth, a type of the Israelites; and in the fact that before
the creation of the sun the waters produced nothing, and
the earth little that was good, while after the sun had
shone upon them they became fruitful abundantly of
moving creatures, birds, and fishes, a prophecy of the
spiritual revolution wrought by Christianity—were not
the Apostles fishers of men? and a plain, unmistakable
proof that his exposition is no mere fancy, but solid
truth. It is absurd to criticize such folly seriously, but it
may be worth while to note in passing that Christ being
according to Christian theology co-eternal with the Father,
the creation of the sun serves but ill as a type of His
advent.

Pico, however, is so little disturbed by this considera-
tion, that he finds another type of Christ in another
created object — to wit, the firmament — which, while
separating the waters above it from those below, nevertheless unites them as every mean unites its extremes,
and thus enables the former to fecundate the latter, as
Christ enables the divine grace to descend upon man.
At the same time, however, he is careful to affirm the
orthodox position that Christ is the first begotten of every
creature.

Such are some of the meanings which Pico finds in the
Mosaic text when interpreting it of the creation of the
intelligible or super-celestial sphere. The same terms
have, of course, quite different imports when applied to
the creation of the other spheres. Thus, in relation to
the sublunary sphere, "heaven" means efficient cause,
"the earth" matter, and "the waters" on the face of

which the Spirit of God moved, the accidents of matter.

But the reader has probably had already far too much of these absurdities, which, however, when due allowance has been made for the differences of the times, are perhaps hardly grosser than some of the ingenious attempts by which more recent writers have sought to reconcile Genesis with modern science.

It is time, however, to take a glance at the treatise "De Ente et Uno." This little tractate purports to be an essay towards the reconciliation of Plato and Aristotle —an essentially hopeless undertaking, on which Poryhyry had long before spent his strength for nought. We may therefore spare ourselves the trouble of even asking how far Pico is successful. The interest of the treatise consists in the insight which it affords into Pico's own views of the nature of God and His relation to the world. It is, in fact, a chapter, and by no means an unimportant chapter, in the long dialectic on the nature of universals and their relation to particulars, which formed the staple of mediæval thought. All cultivated people have heard of this great debate, but few have any clear idea of the issues involved in it, and why so many subtle and ingenious thinkers spent their best energies upon it. Nay, it is sometimes contemptuously dismissed by those who should know better as mere piece of frivolous logomachy. In truth, however, this apparently barren controversy was big with the most momentous of all the problems with which the human mind can concern itself—first, " Utrum sit Deus "—whether God exist ? second, if He exist, in what way His relation to the universe is to be understood—whether in the way of a transcendent cause or an immanent principle, or in both ways at once ?

Saturated as mediæval theology was with ideas derived from Plato and Aristotle, and but imperfectly understood, it was inevitable that when men attempted to philosophize about God, they should conceive Him—or at any rate tend to conceive Him—rather as a universal principle, or archetypal source of ideas, than as a concrete personality.   Hence nominalism, with its frank denial of the existence of universals, conceptualism with its reduction of them to figments of abstraction, seemed equally to involve atheism; even realism of the more moderate type, which, while asserting the objective existence of the universal, denied its existence *ante rem*—*i.e.*, apart from the particular—was viewed with suspicion as tending to merge God in the cosmos; while realism of the high Platonic order, by its assertion of the existence of a world of pure universals—archetypes of the particulars revealed to sense—found favour in the eyes of men in whom the philosophic interest was always strictly subordinated to the theological.

In the treatise " De Ente et Uno " the question as between the transcendence and the immanence of God comes to the surface with remarkable abruptness.   Is "the One," *i.e.* God, to be regarded as " Being " or as "above Being ?" Aristotle is supposed to maintain the former position, Plato undoubtedly holds the latter.   To the Platonic doctrine Pico gives in his unqualified adhesion, and attempts to constrain Aristotle to do so likewise.   His Platonism is of the most uncompromising type, the idealism of the Parmenides with the Parmenidean doubts and difficulties left out.   Abstract terms such as " whiteness " or " humanity " signify, he asserts dogmatically, and apparently without a shadow of doubt as to the truth of the doctrine, real existences which are what they are in their own right

and not by derivation from or participation in anything
else, while their corresponding concretes denote existences
of an inferior order which are what they are by virtue of
their participation in the abstract or archetypal ideas.
Upon this theory he proceeds deliberately to base his
theology. As whiteness in itself is not white, but the
archetypal cause of that particular appearance in objects,
and in the same way heat in itself is not hot, but the cause
of the particular sensation which we call heat; so God is
not " Being" though, or rather because, He is the "fulness,"
i.e. the archetypal cause, of " Being." As thus the one
primal fountain of " Being " He is properly described as
" the One." " God is all things and most eminently and
most perfectly all things; which cannot be, unless He so
comprehends the perfections of all things in Himself as to
exclude whatever imperfection is in them. Now, things
are imperfect either (1) in virtue of some defect in themselves, whereby they fall short of the normal standard
proper to them, or (2) in virtue of the very limitations
which constitute them particular objects. It follows that
God being perfect has in Him neither any defect nor any
particularity, but is the abstract universal unity of all
things in their perfection. It is, therefore, not correct to
say that He comprehends all things in Himself; for in
that case neither would He be perfectly simple in nature,
nor would they be infinite which are in Him, but He
would be an infinite unity composed of many things
infinite, indeed, in number, but finite in respect of perfection; which to speak or think of God is profanity."
In other words, in order to get a true idea of God we
must abstract from all plurality, all particularity whatever,
and then we have as the residue the notion of a most
perfect, infinite, perfectly simple being. God may, then,

be called Being itself, the One itself, the Good itself, the
True itself; but it is better to describe Him as that which
is "above Being, above truth, above unity, above goodness, since His Being is truth itself, unity itself, goodness
itself," better still to say of Him that He is "intelligibly
and ineffably above all that we can most perfectly say or
conceive of Him," and with Dionysius the Areopagite
to define him by negatives. And so he quotes with
approval part of the closing sentence of the treatise "De
Mystica Theologia" in which agnosticism seems to exhaust
itself in the exuberant detail of its negations. "It" (*i.e.*
the First Cause) "is neither truth, nor dominion, nor wisdom, nor the One, nor unity, nor Deity, nor goodness, nor
spirit, as far as we can know; nor sonship nor fatherhood,
nor aught else of things known to us or any other creature; neither is it aught of things that are not nor of
things that are; nor is it known to any as it is itself nor
knows them itself as they are; whose is neither speech,
nor name, nor knowledge, nor darkness, nor light, nor
error, nor truth, nor any affirmation or negation." And
then, to give a colour of orthodoxy to his doctrine he
quotes the authority of St. Augustine to the effect that
"the wisdom of God is no more wisdom than justice,
His justice no more justice than wisdom, His life no more
life than cognition, His cognition no more cognition than
life; for all these qualities are united in God not in the
way of confusion or combination or by the interpenetra-
tion as it were of things in themselves distinct, but by way
of a perfectly simple ineffable fontal unity": a summary
statement of some passages in the sixth book of the treatise
" De Trinitate," which is of course misleading apart from
the context in which they occur.

Such is Pico's theory of the Godhead—a theory which

in fact reduces it to the mere abstraction of perfect simplicity and universality, a theory wholly irreconcilable with the Christian faith, wholly unfit to form the basis of religion. Nor was its author insensible, rather he would seem to have been only too painfully conscious of the barrenness of the results to which so much toil and trouble had brought him; for he has no sooner enunciated it than he turns, as if with a sigh, to Politian, and addresses him thus :—" But see, my Angelo, what madness possesses us. Love God while we are in the body we rather may than either define or know Him. By loving Him we more profit ourselves, have less trouble, please Him better. Yet had we rather ever seeking Him by the way of speculation never find Him than by loving Him possess that which without loving were in vain found "—words that since Pico's day must have found an echo in the heart of many a thinker weary with the vain effort to gain by philosophical methods a clear insight into the divine nature.

The treatise involved Pico in an amicable controversy with his friend Antonio da Faenza (Antonius Faventinus or Cittadinus), who criticised it in some detail, and to whom Pico replied with no less detail. The correspondence was protracted during his life, and was continued after his death by his nephew, but it sheds little additional light on Pico's views. How far he seriously held them, and whether he had some esoteric method of reconciling them with the orthodox faith, are questions which we have no means of answering. It is curious, however, in reference to this matter, to compare the opening chapters of his commentary on Girolamo Benivieni's *canzone* on "Celestial Love." Benivieni also was a Platonist, and having saturated himself with the Symposium and the Phædrus, the fifth book of the third Ennead of Plotinus, and Ficino's commentaries, thought himself qualified to write a *canzone* on ideal love which should put Guinicelli and Cavalcanti to shame. The result was that he produced a *canzone* which has a certain undeniable elevation of style, but is so obscure that even with the help of Pico's detailed commentary it takes some hard study to elicit its meaning. The theme, however, is the purifying influence of love in raising the soul through various stages of refinement from the preoccupation with sensuous beauty to the contemplation of the ideal type of the beautiful, and thence to the knowledge of God, who, though, as Pico is careful to explain, He is not beautiful Himself, since beauty implies an element of variety repugnant to His nature, is nevertheless the source of the beautiful no less than of the true and the good.

The commentary consists of two parts; the first a philosophical dissertation on love in general, its nature, origin, and place in the universal scheme of things; the second a detailed analysis and exposition of the poem, stanza by stanza, almost line by line. Both parts, in spite of the good Italian in which they are written, are unspeakably tedious, being mostly made up of bald rationalizations of Greek myths. The first few chapters, however, are theological or theosophical; and here we find God described consistently with the doctrine of the " De Ente et Uno" as "ineffably elevated above all intellect and cognition," while beneath Him, and between the intelligible and the sensible worlds is placed "a creature of nature as perfect as it is possible for a creature to be," whom God creates from eternity, whom alone He immediately creates, and who " by Plato and likewise by the ancient philosophers, Mercury Trismegistus and

Zoroaster is called now the Son of God, now Mind, now Wisdom, now Divine Reason." Here we have a fusion and confusion of the "self-sufficing and most perfect God" created by the Demiurge of Plato's Timæus to be the archetype of the world, the Son of God of Philo and later theosophists, and the Νοῦς of Plotinus, the first emanation of the Godhead. This Son of God, however, Pico bids us observe, is not to be confounded with the Son of God of Christian theology, who is Creator and not creature, but may be regarded as " the first and most noble angel created by God."

This is virtually Pico's last word on theology or theosophy, and it leaves the question of his orthodoxy an insoluble enigma. Did he really believe in the Son of God of Christian theology, or had he not rather dethroned Him in favour of the syncretistic abstraction which he calls the first and most noble angel created by God, though he was too timid to avow the fact. We have seen that he did not scruple to find types of Christ in created things, such as the firmament and the sun. Little stress can be laid on this, and if it stood alone it might be dismissed as a piece of sheer inadvertence, but read in connection with the pregnant passage from the commentary on Benivieni's poem, it certainly makes in favour of the idea that in the passion for unity which evidently possessed him Pico had abandoned his trinitarianism, and that the treatise "De Ente et Uno" contains his most mature and profound theological convictions. If so, the caution against confusing the two Sons of God must be interpreted as a mere device to save appearances.

However this may be, it is undeniable that Pico was, even in the conventional Christian sense, a sincerely religious man. The letter to his nephew, Giovanni

Francesco, on the spiritual life, translated by More, has in it the ring of genuine simple Christian godliness, and though Savonarola saw fit to consign him to the purgatorial fire for his refusal to devote himself entirely to the religious life, he did so probably rather in sorrow than in anger, on the principle that whom the Lord loveth He chasteneth, regarding Pico as one who had in him the making of a saint, but who by a *gran rifiuto* failed of attaining unto the prize of his high calling.

That Pico should have found a theology which reduces God to a *caput mortuum* of which nothing can be said but that it is above all things, and Christ to a "great angel," the first of created beings, compatible with the simple and ardent piety of a Catholic saint would indeed be a notable phenomenon, but, at the same time, one which sound criticism would accept without attempting to account for it, much less to explain it away. No exercise of ingenuity would ever succeed in harmonising his theology with the Catholic or any form of the Christian faith, and it is equally impossible to dispute the sincerity of his piety. It is all part and parcel of the peculiar, unique idiosyncracy of the man's nature, a nature compounded of mysticism and rationalism, credulity and scepticism, in about equal proportions.

He finds strange hidden meanings in the simple words of Moses, he believes in natural magic, and holds that it testifies more clearly of Christ than any other science, yet he cannot credit the story of Christ's descent into hell, or the doctrine of transubstantiation, or the eternity of punishment, and writes an elaborate treatise in twelve books against the pretensions of astrology. A man of immense and varied learning, not merely classical but oriental, he yet permitted himself to be imposed on by a

Sicilian Jew, to whom he gave an immense sum for some worthless cabalistic treatises, under the impression that they were the lost works of Ezra.

Perhaps it is unfair to take seriously what may have been merely a compliment less sincere than gracious ; but it certainly does not tend to raise one's impression of his critical powers to find Pico, in a letter to Lorenzo de' Medici, setting Lorenzo's insipid verses above anything that Dante or Petrarch ever wrote.

With all this it is more easy to do injustice than justice to Pico. It is impossible to study him attentively without seeing at last that amidst all his vagaries, absurdities, perversities, there was real faculty in him, and faculty of an order which, matured by a severer discipline than his age could afford, would have won for him a place, though perhaps no very exalted one, among philosophers. The philosophic instinct, without doubt, he had, and in high measure, a veritable passion not merely for truth but for a consistent, harmonious body of truth. The high originative faculty which discovers a method was denied him. Hence he remained a mere syncretist forlornly struggling to weave the discordant utterances of rival schools into a coherent system. His importance for the student of philosophy is that he made this attempt, made it with wider knowledge and more passionate zeal than any of his predecessors, and failed, and that with his failure scholasticism as a movement came to an end. Individual thinkers indeed there have been, such as Leibniz and Coleridge, in whom something of Pico's spirit has survived, whose laudable anxiety to justify the ways of God to man has led them to attempt the reconciliation of the irreconcilable, of atomism, *e.g.*, with idealism, of transcendentalism with the Christian faith, and such men are in effect schoolmen born out of due time. Nevertheless that which in the specific sense we call scholasticism made in Pico its final effort, was beaten by the sheer intractability of its problem, which the new learning made ever more apparent, and died out.

Schoolman, however, though Pico was, it must not be forgotten that he was also a humanist. His style, even where, as in the "Apologia," he is at his driest and most formal, and in the attempt to reconcile his heresies with Catholic doctrine, becomes, in the fineness of his distinctions, almost more scholastic than the subtlest doctor that ever spun intellectual cobwebs in Oxford or Paris, effectually distinguishes him from "the barbarians," and proclaims him a child of the renaissance; and long and justly celebrated were the "golden letters" in which, in all the luxuriance of Ciceronic periods, he praises Politian's translation of the *Enchiridion* of Epictetus or Lorenzo's verses, discusses the rival claims of the old and new learning with Ermolao Barbaro, descants on the regal dignity of philosophy and philosophers to Andrea Corneo, exhorts his nephew to the practice of the Christian life, or expatiates to Ficino on his new-born zeal for oriental studies.

In none of these does he appear to better advantage than in one of the earliest, written in reply to a flattering letter from Politian, which in effect admitted him to the confraternity of learned men.

"I am as much beholden to you," he writes, "for the high praise you give me in your last letter as I am far from deserving it. For one is beholden to another for what he gives, not for what he pays. Wherefore, indeed, I am beholden to you for all that you write of me, since in me there is nothing of the kind, for you in no way owed it to me, but it all came of your courtesy and singular graciousness towards me. For the rest, if you examine me, you will find nothing in me that is not slight, humble, strictly limited. I am a novice, a tiro, and have advanced but a step, no more, from the darkness of ignorance. It is a compliment to place me in the rank of a student. Something more is meant by a man of learning, a title appropriate only to you and your likes, too grand for me; since of those matters which in letters are most important I have as yet obtained no thorough knowledge, scarcely more indeed than, as it were, a peep through a lattice window. I will endeavour indeed, and that I now do, to become some time or another such as you say and either really think, or at any rate would fain think, that I am. Meantime I will follow your example, Angelo, who excuse yourself to the Greeks by the fact that you are a Latin, to the Latins on the ground that you grecize. I too will have recourse to a similar subterfuge, and claim the indulgence of the poets and rhetoricians because I am said to philosophize, of the philosophers because I play the rhetorician and cultivate the Muses; though my case is very different from yours. For in sooth while I desire to sit, as they say, on two chairs, I fall between them, and it turns out at last (to be brief) that I am neither a poet, nor a rhetorician, nor a philosopher." How strictly these gloomy forebodings were realised in the matter of philosophy we have already seen. From attempting to decide how far his cultivation of the Muses was rewarded we are precluded by Pico's own act, the destruction of his early love poems. Of these the following sonnet alone has been preserved :—

Da poi che i duo belli occhi che mi fanno
Cantar del mio Signor sì nuovamente,
Avvamparo la mia gelata mente,
Già volge in lieta sorte il second' anno.

xxx

> Felice giorno, ch'a sì dolce affanno
>   Fu bel principio ; onde nel cor si sente
>   Una fiamma girar sì dolcemente,
>   Che men beati son que' che 'n ciel stanno.
>
> L'ombra, il pensier, la negligenza, e'l letto
>   M'avean ridotto, ove la maggior parte
>   Giace ad ogn' or del vulgo errante e vile.
>
> Scorsemi Amore a più gradito oggetto :
>   E se cosa di grato oggi a 'l mio stile,
>   Madonna affina in me l'ingegno e l'arte.

> Since first the light of those twin stars, thine eyes,
>   That me to hymn my Lord thus newly move,
>   Kindled my frost-bound soul with fires of love,
>   Years twain their course have run in happy wise.
>
> O blessed day, of such sweet heaviness
>   Such fair beginning !   Since when to and fro
>   Within my heart a gentle flame doth go,
>   That not in heaven is found such happiness.
>
> Recluse I lived, in musing lost, nor care,
>   Nor action knew, wellnigh become a part
>   Of the vile herd of errant men and base.
>
> Love roused my soul to seek an end more fair :
>   And if my style to-day has aught of grace
>   My lady 'tis refines my mind and art.

If this somewhat insipid sonnet is a fair sample of Pico's amatory effusions, one can more readily understand why he burned them than the regret which their destruction caused Politian, and which drew from him the following epigram :—

> Πολλάκι τοξευθεὶς φλεχθείς θ' ὑπὸ Πίκος ἐρώτων
>   Οὐκ ἔτλη προτέρῳ, πάντα δ'ἀφείλεθ' ὅπλα,
> Τόξα, βέλη, φαρέτρας, καὶ νήσας τά γε πάντα
>   Ἥψεν ὁμοῦ σωρὸν λαμπάσι λῃιδίοις.
> Σὺν δ'αὐτοὺς μάρψας ἀμενηνὰ χερύδρια δῆσεν
>   Ταῖς νευραῖς, μέσσῃ δ' ἔμβαλε πυρκαϊᾷ.
> Καὶ πυρὶ φλέξε τὸ πῦρ· τί δ ὦ ἄφρονες αὐτὸν ἔρωτες
>   Τὸν Πίκον μουσῶν εἰσεποτᾶσθε πρόμον ;

Ficino took a different view from Politian. "Somewhat
of love," he wrote after Pico's death, "he had written in the
heat of his youth, which in his riper judgment he con-
demned and determined altogether to destroy, nor could
it have been published without damage to his reputation."
This, however, probably refers not so much to the literary merit of the poems as to their moral tone. His
nephew, Giovanni Francesco Pico distinctly states that
they were destroyed "religionis causa." It is evident
also from the way in which Politian refers to them that
they were such as a less severe moralist than Ficino
might have censured. "I hear," he wrote, "that you
have burned the little love poems which you made in the
past, fearing perhaps lest they should injure your fair
fame or the morals of others. For I cannot think that
you have destroyed them, as Plato is said to have destroyed
his, because they were not worthy of publication. For
as far as I remember nothing could be more terse, more
sweet or more polished." Pico was wont to solace himself
with Propertius, and had wantoned with other ladies than
the Muses, so that in all likelihood his love poetry was
decidedly more ardent than chaste. More (p. 13 *infra*) is
inaccurate in stating that the "five books" thus destroyed
were in the vulgar tongue. They were written, as we
learn from Giovanni Francesco Pico "elegiaco carmine,"
i.e. in Latin elegies, probably modelled on Propertius.
The Italian poems, however, were destroyed at the same
time. Of Pico's Latin elegiacs two specimens survive:
(1) a hymn to God written probably after his conversion;
(2) an encomiastic poem on his friend Girolamo Benivieni.
For the first no high merit can be claimed. The attempt
to give poetical expression to the mysteries of Christian
theology is nearly always unsuccessful, and Pico's "Depre-

catoria" forms no exception to the rule. The most that can be said for it is that it is tolerable Latin. Such as it is, however, it is here printed for comparison with More's translation, which will be found at page 74 *infra*.

JOANNIS PICI MIRANDULÆ DEPRECATORIA AD DEUM.

Alme Deus ! summa qui majestate verendus,
    Vere unum in triplici numine numen habes :
Cui super excelsi flammantia mœnia mundi
    Angelici servit turba beata chori :
Cujus et immensum hoc oculis spectabile nostris
    Omnipotens quondam dextra creavit opus :
Æthera qui torques, qui nutu dirigis orbem,
    Cujus ab imperio fulmina missa cadunt :
Parce, precor, miseris, nostras, precor, ablue sordes,
    Ne nos justa tui pœna furoris agat.
Quod si nostra pari pensentur debita lance
    Et sit judicii norma severa tui,
Quis queat horrendum viventis ferre flagellum
    Vindicis, et plagas sustinuisse graves ?
Non ipsa iratæ restabit Machina dextræ,
    Machina supremo non peritura die.
Quæ mens non primæ damnata ab origine culpæ,
    Aut quæ non proprio crimine facta nocens ?
Ast certe ille ipse es proprium cui parcere semper,
    Justitiamque pari qui pietate tenes :
Præmia qui ut meritis longe maiora rependis,
    Supplicia admissis sic leviora malis.
Namque tua est nostris major clementia culpis,
    Et dare non dignis res mage digna Deo est.
Quamquam sat digni, si quos dignatur amare
    Qui quos non dignos invenit ipse facit.
Ergo tuos placido miserans, precor, aspice vultu,
    Seu servos mavis, seu magis esse reos :
Nempe reos, nostræ si spectes crimina vitæ,
    Ingratæ nimium crimina mentis opus :
At tua si potius in nobis munera cernas,
    Munera præcipuis nobilitata bonis,
Nos sumus ipsa olim tibi quos natura ministros
    Mox fecit natos gratia sancta tuos.

Sed premit heu ! miseros tantæ indulgentia sortis,
    Quos fecit natos gratia, culpa reos.
Culpa reos fecit, sed vincat gratia culpam,
    Ut tuus in nostro crimine crescat honor.
Nam tua sive aliter sapientia, sive potestas,
    Nota suas mundo prodere possit opes,
Major in erratis bonitatis gloria nostris,
    Illeque præ cunctis fulget amandus amor,
Qui potuit cœlo Dominum deducere ab alto,
    Inque crucem summi tollere membra Dei :
Ut male contractas patrio de semine sordes
    Ablueret lateris sanguis et unda tui :
Sic amor et pietas tua, Rex mitissime, tantis
    Dat mala materiem suppeditare bonis.
O amor ! O pietas nostris bene provida rebus !
    O bonitas servi facta ministra tui !
O amor ! O pietas nostris male cognita sæclis !
    O bonitas nostris nunc prope victa malis !
Da, precor, huic tanto qui semper fervet amori
    Ardorem in nostris cordibus esse parem :
Da Sathanæ imperium, cui tot servisse per annos
    Pœnitet excusso deposuisse jûgo :
Da, precor, extingui vesanæ incendia mentis,
    Et tuus in nostro pectore vivat amor :
Ut cum mortalis perfunctus munere vitæ
    Ductus erit Dominum spiritus ante suum,
Promissi regni felici sorte potitus
    Non Dominum sed Te sentiat esse Patrem.

The poem on Benivieni is in a happier vein :—

Lætor, io, Tyrrhena, tibi, Florentia, lætor !
    Clamet, io Pæan, quisquis amicus adest !
Quale decus, quæ fama, tibi, quæ gloria surgit !
    Tolle caput, Libycas tolle superba jubas !
Ille tuos agros intra et tua mœnia natus,
    Atque Arni liquidas inter adultus aquas,
Cui cum divinum sit sacro in pectore numen
    Quam bene de sacro nomine nomen habet !
Ille, inquam, plausu jam cœpit ubique frequenti,
    Jam cœpit multo non sine honore legi.
Sicelis Ausonias illius Musa per urbes
    Fert celebrem magna candida laude pedem.

Auctorem patriæ quisquis legit invidet illi,
      Atque optat patriæ nomina tanta suæ.
Gaude, gaude iterum tanto insignita decore,
      Et vati adplaudas terra beata tuo.
Cinge coronatos vernanti flore capillos,
      Conveniunt titulo Florida serta tuo.
Undique Achæmenio spargantur compita costo,
      Et per odoratas lilia multa vias.
En ! stirps in nostras Benivenia protulit auras
      Etruscum docto qui gerat ore senem !
Ponite Avernales jam gens Etrusca cupressus,
      Quas rapta immiti funere Laura dedit.
Pellantur queruli fletus ; en ! Laura revixit ;
      Spirat ; et argutum novit, ut ante, loqui.
Quin solito nitet illa magis, majorque priore
      Nescio quæ cultu gratia ab ore venit.
Reddidit hanc nobis laus nostræ Hieronimus urbis,
      Et dedit infernos posse iterare lacus :
At certe (procul hinc O Livor inique facessas)
      Nunc graviore sonat grandius illa chely.
Di Superi ! sublime ales modulatur, ut æqua
      Sit jam Romano Tusca loquela sono.
Nec tamen ille Euros frondosus jactat inanes :
      Plus quam promittit fronte recessus habet.
Quid referam, quam lenis erat ? quam carmina plano
      In numeros currunt ordine juncta suos :
Sic memini me sæpe sacros vidisse liquores
      Profluere, imbriferi vis ubi nulla Noti.
Sed quis miretur meditato in carmine tantum
      Cultus, cum pariter non meditata canat ?
Quis non hunc juret Phœbum, modo pendeat arcus ?
      Cornua sint, Bromium quis neget esse Deum ?
Audivi hunc quoties cithara cantare recurva,
      Abduxit sensus protinus ille meos.
Et quid non possent digiti mulcere loquentis ?
      Sisteret his rapidi flumina magna Padi :
Phœbeos medio firmaret in æthere currus :
      Lunares pictos sisteret axe boves.
Terribilem sævis Martem revocaret ab armis :
      Leniret Ditem, falciferumque senem :
Et quas non potuit quondam Rhodopeius Orpheus
      Flectere Strymonias flecteret ille nurus.

XXXV

The poem was apparently written after the death of Lorenzo, whose successor Pico hails in Benivieni. The epithet "Sicelis," applied to Benivieni's muse, refers to his bucolics; one of which (in praise of poetry) is entitled "Lauro," after Lorenzo; in another, which bears the name of "Pico," Lorenzo and Pico converse in amœbean strains. "Laura" stands apparently for Lorenzo's muse. "Etruscum qui gerat ore senem," is an uncouth and somewhat obscure phrase. "Nec tamen ille Euros frondosus jactat inanes" is plainly corrupt, but it is not easy to suggest a satisfactory emendation. "Quid referam, quam lenis *erat?*" is too bad Latin to have been written by Pico. Perhaps the true reading is "quam lene sonet." The verses are undeniably spirited, though somewhat too rhetorical for true poetry.

It is, indeed, only as a rhetorician that Pico can claim to have succeeded. The letter to Ermolao Barbaro in defence of the schoolmen, and that to Lorenzo in praise of his verses are admirable examples of the rhetorical exercise pure and simple — for as such they must primarily be regarded—a little too elaborate, perhaps, too artificial, too declamatory, but still decidedly meritorious in their kind. The air of sincerity they certainly have not—indeed the scholastics of Padua were so far from taking Pico's eloquent panegyric of their predecessors seriously that they were inclined to suspect him of laughing at them in his sleeve. Nor is it easy to believe that Pico was really sincere in the exaggerated encomium which he passed on the verses of Lorenzo, one of the most insipid writers which even that age of learned insipidity produced. The real man, however, undoubtedly speaks in the letters on the philosophic and Christian life, the latter written, it must be remembered, when Pico

was solemnized by the recent death of Lorenzo. The
minor letters exhibit Pico in the pleasant light of the
scholar writing to his friends to give or solicit information
on various literary questions. One closes them, however, with a sigh of regret that the scholar should pre-
dominate so much over the man.

How thankful we should have been for a few easy
gossiping letters in the vulgar tongue revealing Pico to
us as he was in his moments of complete *abandon*. Perhaps, however, he knew none such, and there was nothing
to reveal that he has not revealed. Sense of humour he
seems certainly to have lacked; I have not found in him
the least suggestion that he had any faculty of hearty
laughing in him at all. If he ever had it, severe study
must have crushed it out of him. Probably the basis of
his nature was a deep religious melancholy, not at all
lightened by the fact that learning had impaired his hold
on the faith.

As his short life drew towards its close Pico's preoccupation with religion became more intense and ex-
clusive. Besides the "Rules" of a Christian Life, and
the "Interpretation" of Psalm XVI., translated by More,
he wrote an Exposition of the Lord's Prayer, and pro-
jected, but did not live to execute a Commentary on
the New Testament, for which he prepared himself by
diligent collation of such MSS. as he could come by;
also a defence of the Vulgate and of the Septuagint
version of the Psalms against the criticisms of the Jewish
scholars, and an elaborate apology for Christianity against
seven classes of opponents; to wit (1) atheists, (2)
idolators, (3) Jews, (4) Mahometans, (5) Christians who
reject a portion of the faith, (6) Christians who adulterate
the faith with profane superstitions, (7) orthodox Chris-

tians who live unholy lives. Some idea of the scale of this vast undertaking may be gathered from the fact that the treatise "Adversus Astrologos," which occupies 240 closely printed folio pages formed only a small fragment of it.

But while thus zealous for the defence of the faith, Pico seems never to have seriously contemplated entering the Church, though often urged to do so not only by Savonarola but by other of his friends, who thought he might reasonably aspire to the dignity of cardinal. Their solicitude for his advancement he rebuked with a haughty "Non sunt cogitationes meæ cogitationes vestræ." Probably he considered that he could render religion truer service in the character of lay advocate than if he were trammelled by clerical offices.

Short as his life was, he survived his three most intimate friends, Lorenzo de' Medici, Ermolao Barbaro, and Politian, all of whom died within the two years 1492-4. Probably the grief caused by this succession of misfortunes had much to do with inducing or aggravating the fever of which he died hardly two months after Politian, on 17th Nov. 1494. The corpse, invested by Savonarola's own hands with the habit of the order of the Frati Predicanti, in which he had ardently desired to enrol Pico during his life, was buried in the church of S. Marco. The tomb was inscribed with the epitaph :

> " Joannes jacet hic Mirandula : cætera norunt
> Et Tagus, et Ganges, forsan et Antipodes."

Ficino, who had been to him " in years as a father, in intimacy as a brother, in affection as a second self," wrote another epitaph, which was not, however, placed upon the tomb : " Antistites secretiora mysteria raro admodum concedunt oculis, statimque recondunt. Ita Deus mortalibus divinum philosophum Joannem Picum Mirandulam trigesimo (*sic*) anno maturum."

The generous enthusiasm which prompted Politian to confer upon his friend the high-sounding title of "Phœnix of the wits" (Fenice degli ingegni) has not been justified by events. Once sunk in his ashes the Phœnix never rose again.

The pious care of Giovanni Francesco Pico, who published his uncle's life and works at Venice in 1498, did much, indeed, to avert the oblivion which ultimately fell upon him. This edition, however, was imperfect, the Theses and the Commentary on Benivieni's poem, with some minor matters being omitted. These were added in the Basel edition of 1601. The "Golden Letters" have passed through many editions, the last that of Cellario in 1682. The Commentary on Celestial and Divine Love was reprinted as late as 1731.

Pico figures in a dim and ever dimmer way in the older histories of philosophy from Stanley, who gives a rude and imperfect translation of the "Commentary" to Hegel, who dismisses him and his works in a few lines. More recently, however, one of Hegel's laborious fellow-countrymen, Georg Dreydorff, discovered a system in Pico and expounded it.[1]

But most Englishmen probably owe such interest as he excites in them to Mr. Pater's charming sketch in his dainty volume of studies entitled "The Renaissance," or the slighter notices in Mr. J. A. Symonds' "Renaissance in Italy," or Mr. Seebohm's "Oxford Reformers."

The Life by Sir Thomas More now reprinted is a

[1] "Das System des Johann Pico Grafen von Mirandula und Concordia," *Marburg*, 1858.

somewhat reduced and inaccurate version of Giovanni Francesco Pico's work. The reprint is executed from a small black-letter quarto in the British Museum, printed by Wynkyn de Worde about 1510. The old spelling and, as far as possible, the old punctuation has been retained, though in many places it has been necessary to alter the latter in order to avoid intolerable harshness or obscurity.

The chronicles of Mirandola, edited for the municipality in 1872, under the title " Memorie Storiche della Città e dell' Antico Ducato della Mirandola," are an authority of capital importance for the history of the Pico family and its connexions. The notes to Riccardo Bartoli's " Elogio al Principe Pico " (1791) also contain some valuable original matter. The critical judgment of the last century on Pico's services to the cause of the revival of learning is given by Christoph Meiners in " Lebensbeschreibungen berühmter Männer der Wiederherstellung der Wissenschaften." Some of Pico's letters translated, into the ponderous English of the period, connected by a thread of biography, and illustrated by erudite notes, will be found in W. Parr Greswell's " Memoirs of Angelus Politianus," etc. 1805. The best modern Italian biography is that by F. Calori Cesis, entitled " Giovanni Pico della Mirandola detto La Fenice degli Ingegni " (2nd edn. 1872).

HERE IS CONTEYNED THE LYFE OF JOHAN PICUS
ERLE OF MYRANDULA A GRETE LORDE OF
ITALY AN EXCELLENT CONNYNGE MAN IN ALL
SCIENCES & VERTEOUS OF LYVYNGE. WITH
DYVERS EPYSTLES & OTHER WERKES OF Y^E
SAYD JOHAN PICUS FULL OF GRETE SCIENCE
VERTUE & WYSEDOME WHOSE LIFE &
WERKES BENE WORTHY & DYGNE
TO BE REDDE AND OFTEN
TO BE HAD IN
MEMORYE.

UNTO HIS RYGHT ENTYERLY BELOVED
SYSTER IN CHRYST JOYEUCE LEYGH[1]
THOMAS MORE GRETYNG IN OUR LORDE.

IT is and of longe tyme hath bene my
well beloved ſyſter a cuſtome in the
begynnynge of yᵉ newe yere frendes to
ſende betwene preſentes or gyſtes, as
the wytneſſes of theyr love and ſrende
ſhyp & alſo ſygnyſyenge that they deſyre
eche to other that yere a good contynuance and proſperous
ende of that lucky bygynnynge. But communely all
thoſe preſentes that are uſed cuſtomably all in this maner
betwene frendes to be ſente be ſuche thynges as pertayne
onely unto the body eyther to be fed or to be cledde or
ſome otherwyſe delyted : by whiche hit ſemeth that theyr
frendſhyp is but fleſſhely & ſtretcheth in maner to the
body onely. But for aſmoche as the love & amyte of
chryſten folke ſholde be rather gooſty frendſhyp then
bodely : ſyth yᵗ all faythfull people are rather ſpyrituall
then carnall : for as th'apoſtle ſeyth we be not now in
fleſſhe but in ſpyryte yf Chryſte abyde in us : I therfore
myne hertly beloved ſyſter in good lucke of this newe
yere have ſent you ſuche a preſent as maye bere wytnes
of my tendre love & zele to the happy contynuaunce and
gracyouſe encreace of vertue in your ſoule : and where as

3

the giftes of other folke declare y' they wyfsheth theyr
frendes to be worldly fortunate, myne teftyfyeth y' I defyre to have you godly profperous.   Thefe werkes more
profitable then large were made in laten by one Johan Picus
Erle of Mirandula a lordfhyp in Italy, of whose connynge
& vertue we nede here nothinge to fpeke, for afmoche as
here after we perufe the courfe of his hole lyfe rather after
our lytel power flenderly then after his merites fuffyciently.
The werkes are fuche that truely good fyfter I fuppofe of
the quantyte there cometh none in your hand more profitable : neyther to th'achyvynge of temperaunce in pro-
fperite, nor to y⁰ purchafynge of pacience in adverfite,
nor to the dyfpyfynge of worldly vanyte, nor to the defyrynge of hevenly felycyte : whiche werkes I wolde
requyre you gladly to receyve : ne were hit y' they be
fuche that for the goodly mater (how fo ever they be
tranflated) may delyte & pleafe ony perfone that hath
ony meane defyre and love to God : and that your felfe
is fuche one as for your vertue and fervent zele to God
can not but joyoufly receyve ony thynge that meanely
fowneth eyther to the reproche of vyce, commendacyon
of vertue, or honoure and laude of God, who preferve
you.

THE LYFE OF JOHAN PICUS, ERLE OF MIRANDULA.

OHAN PICUS OF THE faders[2] fyde defcended of the worthy lynage of th'emperoure Conftantyne by a nevew of the fayd Emperour called Picus, by whom all the Aunceftres of this Johan Picus undoubtedly bere that name. But we fhal let his aunceftres paffe, to whome (though they were ryght excellent) he gave agayne as moche honour as he receyved. And we fhal fpeke of hym felfe reherfynge in parte his lernynge and his vertue. For thefe be the thynges whiche maye accompte for our owne, of whiche every man is more proprely to be commended then of ye noblenes of his aunceftres: whofe honoure maketh us not honorable. For eyther they were them felfe vertuoufe or not: yf not, then had they none honour them felfe had they never fo grete poffeffyons: for honoure is the rewarde of vertue. And how may they clayme the rewarde y^t proprely longeth to vertue: yf they lak the vertue that ye rewarde longeth to. Then yf them felfe had none honour: how myght they leve to theyr heyres y^t thynge whiche they had not them felfe. On ye other fyde yf they be vertuous and fo confequently

5

honorable, yet maye they not leve theyr honoure to us as
enheretaunce : no more then the vertue that them felfe
were honourable for. For never the more noble be we
for theyr noblenes : yf our felfe lak thofe thynges for
which they were noble. But rather the more worfhipful
that our aunceftres were, the more vile and fhamfull be
we : yf we declyne from yᵉ fteppes of theyr worfhypfull
lyvynge : yᵉ clere beauty of whofe vertue makith the
darke fpotte of our vyce the more evydently to appere
and to be yᵉ more marked. But Picus of whom we fpeke
was him felfe fo honorable, for yᵉ grete plentuoufe
habundaunce of all fuche vertues, yᵉ poffeffyon wherof
very honoure foloweth (as a fhadowe folowith a body)
yᵗ he was to all them yᵗ afpyre to honour a very fpectacle,
in whofe condycyons as in a clere pullifhed myrrour they
myght beholde in what poyntes very honour ftondeth :
whofe merveylous connynge & excellent vertue though
my rude lernynge be ferre unable fuffyciently to ex-
preffe : yet for as moche as yf no man fholde do hit but
he yᵗ might fufficiently do hit, no man fholde do hit : &
better it were to be unfufficiently done then utterly un-
done : I fhal therfore as I can brefely reherfe you his
hole lyfe : at the leeft wyfe to gyve fome other man here
after (yᵗ can do hit better) occafyon to take hit in hande
when hit fhall happely greve hym to fe the lyfe of fuche
an excellent connyng man fo ferre unkonnyngly wryten.

OF HIS PARENTES AND
TYME OF HIS BYRTH.

In yᵉ yere of our Lorde God . M . CCCC . lxiii . Pius the
feconde beynge than the generall vycare of Chryfte in his
chyrche : and Frederyk the thyrde of yᵗ name rulynge
the empyre : this noble man was borne the laft chylde of

his mother Julya, a woman comen of a noble ſtok,[3] his father hyght Johan Fraunciſe, a lorde of grete honoure and auctorite.

OF THE WONDRE THAT APPERED BEFORE HIS BYRTH.

A merveylouſe ſyght was there ſcene before his byrthe : there appered a fyery garlande ſtandynge over yᵉ chaumbre of his mother whyle ſhe travelled & ſodenly vanyſshed away : which apparence was peradventure a token that he whiche ſholde yᵗ houre in the companye of mortall men be borne in the perfeccion of underſtandynge ſholde be lyke yᵉ perfyte fygure of that rounde cyrcle or garlande : and that his excellent name ſholde rounde aboute the cyrcle of this hole world be magnyfyed, whoſe mynde ſholde alway as the fyre aſpyre upwarde to hevenly thynge, and whoſe fyry eloquence ſholde with an ardent hert in tyme to come whorſhip and prayſe almighty God with all his ſtrength : and as that flame ſodenly vaniſshyd ſo ſholde this fyre ſone frome yᵉ eyen of mortal people be hydde. We have oftyntymes red that ſuche unknowen and ſtraunge tokens hathe gone before or foloweth the natyvytefe of excellente wyſe and vertuouſe men, departynge (as hit were) and by Goddes commaundement ſeverynge the cradyls of ſuche ſpecyall chyldren fro yᵉ company of other of the comune ſorte : and ſhewynge yᵗ they be borne to the acchevynge of ſome grete thyng. But to paſſe over other. The grete Saynt Ambroſe : a ſwarme of bees flewe aboute his mouth in his cradle, & ſome entred in to his mouthe, and after yᵗ yſſuynge out agayne and fleynge up on hyghe, hydynge them ſelfe amonge the cloudes, eſcaped bothe yᵉ fyght of his father and of all them that were preſent : whiche pronoſtycacyon one

Paulinus [4] makynge moche of, expowned it to fignyfye to us the fwete hony combes of his plefaunt wrytynge: whiche fholde fhewe out the celeftiall gyftes of God & fholde lyfte up the mynde of men from erthe in to heven.

OF HIS PERSONE.

He was of feture and fhappe femely and beauteous, of ftature goodly and hyghe, of flefshe tendre and fofte: his vyfage lovely and fayre, his coloure white entermengled with comely ruddes, his eyen gray and quicke of loke, his teth white and even, his heere yelowe and not to piked. [5]

OF HIS SETTYNGE FORTHE TO SCOLE AND STUDY IN HUMANTYE.

Under y[e] rule and governaunce of his mother he was fet to mayfters & to lernynge: where with fo ardent mynde he labored the ftudyes of humanite: y[t] within fhorte whyle he was (and not without a caufe) accompted amonge the chyef Oratours and Poetes of that tyme: in lernynge mervayloufly fwyfte and of fo redy a wyt, that y[e] verfis whiche he herde ones red he wolde agayne bothe forwarde and bakwarde to the grete wonder of the herers reherfe, and over that wolde holde hit in fure remembraunce: whiche in other folkes wonte comenly to happen contrary. For they y[t] are fwyfte in takyng be oftentymes flowe in remembrynge, and they y[t] with more labour & dyffyculte receyve hit more faft & fuerely holde hit.

OF HIS STUDY IN CANONE.

In the fouretene yere of his age by the commaundement of his mother (whiche longed vere fore to have hym preeft) he departed to Bononye to ftudy in y[e] lawes of the chyrche, whiche whan he had two yere tafted, per-

ceyvynge that the faculte leyned to nothinge but onely
mery tradicions and ordinaunces, his mynde fyll frome
hit : yet loſt he not his tyme therin, for in that two yere
yet beynge a chylde he compyled a brevyary or a ſumme
upon all the decretalles, in whiche as brefly as poſſyble
was he compryſed th' effecte of all yᵗ hole grete volume,
and made a boke no ſclender thyng to ryght connyng &
perfyte doctours.

OF HIS STUDY IN PHYLOSOPHYE
& DEVYNYTE.

After this as a deſyrous enſerchour of the ſecretes of
nature he lefte theſe commyn troden pathes and gave
hym ſelfe hole to ſpeculation & philoſophy as well humane
as devyne. For the purchaſynge wherof (afte the maner
of Plato and Appollonius) [6] he ſcrupulouſly ſought out all
the famous doctours of his tyme, viſytynge ſtudeouſly
all the unyverſytes and ſcoles not onely through Italy but
alſo through Fraunce. And ſo infatigable laboure gave
he to thoſe ſtudies : that yet a chylde and berdles he was
bothe reputed and was in dede bothe a perfyte philoſophre and a perfyte devyne.

OF HIS MYNDE AND VAYNGLORYOUSE
DISPICIONS OF ROME.

Now had he ben. vii. yere converſaunt in theſe ſtudies
whan full of pryde & deſyrous of glory and mannes prayſe
(for yet was he not kendled in yᵉ love of God) he went to
Rome, and there (covetynge to make a shew of his connynge : & lytel conſideringe how grete envye he ſholde
reyſe agaynſt hym ſelfe) ix. C. queſtions he purpoſed, of
dyverſe & ſondry maters : as well in logike and phi-
loſophye as dyvynyte with grete ſtudy piked and ſought

9   c

out as well of the laten auctours as the Grekes : and partly
set oute of the secrete misteryes of the Hebrewes, Caldeyes,
& Arabies : and many thynges drawen out of y⁰ olde obscure philosophye of Pythagoras, Trimegistus, and Orpheus,[7]
& many other thynges straunge : and to all folke (except
ryght fewe specyall excellente men) before that daye : not
unknowen onely : but also unherde of. All whiche questions
in open places (y' they myght be to all people y⁰ better
knowen) he fastened and set up, offeryng also hym selfe
to bere the costes of all suche as wolde come hyther out
of ferre countrees to dyspute, but thorughe y⁰ envye of
his malicyous enemyes (which envye lyke y⁰ fyre ever
draweth to y⁰ hygheft) he coude never brynge a boute to
have a day to his dyspicions appoynted. For this cause
he taryed at Rome an hole yere, in all which tyme his
envyours never durste openly with open dispicyons at-
empt hym, but rather with crafte and sleyght and as it
were with pryvey trenches enforced to under myne hym,
for none other cause but for malice and for they were (as
many men thought) corrupte with a pestylent envye.

This envye as men demed was specyaly raysed agaynst
hym for this cause that where there were many whiche had
many yeres : some for glory : some for couetyse : gyven
them selfe to lernynge : they thought that hit sholde
happely deface theyr fame & minysshe th'opynyon of
theyr connynge yf so yonge a man plenteouse of sub-
staunce & greate doctryne durste in the chyefe cyte of
the worlde make a profe of his wyt and his lernyng : as
well in thinges naturall as in divinite & in many suche
thynges as men many yeres never attayned to. Nowe
when they perceyved that they coude not agaynst his
connynge ony thynge openly preuayle, they brought
forth the serpentynes of false crime, and cryed out that

there wer. xiij. of his. ix. C. queſtyons ſuſpecte of heryſye.
Then joyned they to them ſome good ſymple folke that
ſholde of zele to yᵉ fayth and pretence of relygion im-
pugne thoſe queſtions as newe thynges & with whiche
theyr eres had not be in ure. In whiche impugnacyon
though ſome of theym happely lacked not good mynde:
yet lacked they erudycyon and lernynge: whiche queſtyons notwitſtondynge before that not a ſewe famous
doctours of divynyte had approved as good and clene,
and ſubſcribed theyr names undre them. But he not
berynge the loſſe of his fame made a defence for. thoſe
xiij. queſtyons: a werke of greate erudicyon and elegant
and ſtuffed with the cognytyon of many thynges worthy
to be lerned. Whiche werke he compyled in xx nyghtes.
In whiche hit evedently appereth: not onely that thoſe
concluſyons were good and ſtondyng with the ſayth: but
alſo yᵗ they whiche had barked at theym were of ſoly
and rudeneſſe to be reproved: whiche defence and all
other thynges that he ſholde wryte he commytted lyke
a good chryſten man to yᵉ moſt holy judgement of our
mother holy chyrche: whiche defence receyved: & yᵉ xiij.
queſtions duly by delyberacyon examyned: our holy father
yᵉ pope approved Picus and tenderly favoured hym, as by
a bull of our holy father pope Alexandre the vj, hit
playnly appereth: but the boke in whiche the hole. ix. C.
queſtions with theyr concluſions were conteyned (for as
moche as there were in them many thynges ſtraunge and
not fully declared, and were more mete for ſecrete com-
munycacyon of lerned men then for open herynge of
commune people, whiche for lacke of connynge myght
take hurte therby) Picus deſyred hym ſelfe yᵗ hit ſholde
not be redde. And ſoo was the redynge therof forboden.
Lo this ende had Picus of his hye mynde and proud pur-

pofe, that where he thought to have goten perpetual
prayfe there had he moche werke to kepe hymfelfe
upryght: that he ranne not in perpetual infamye and
fclaundre.

OF THE CHAUNGE OF HIS LYFE.

But as hym felfe tolde his nevewe he judged y' this came
thus to paffe: by the efpeciall provifion and fynguler
goodnes of almyghty God, that by this fals cryme untruely
put upon hym by his evyll wyllers he sholde correcte his
very errours, and that this fholde be to hym (wanderynge
in derkenes) as a fhynynge lyght: in whiche he myght
beholde & confydre: how ferre he had gone out of y°
waye of trouth. For before this he had bene bothe
defyrous of glory and kyndled in vayne love and
holden in volupteoufe ufe of women. The comelynes
of his body with the lovely favoure of his vyfage, and
therwith all his merveyloufe fame, his excellent lernynge,
grete rycheffe and noble kyndred, fet many women a fyre
on hym, frome y° defyre of whome he not abhorrynge (y°
waye of lyfe fet a fyde) was fom what fallen in to wanton-
neffe. But after that he was ones with this variaunce
wakened he drewe backe his mynde flowynge in riot &
turned hit to Chryft, womens blandimentes he chaunged
into y° defyre of hevenly joyes, & difpifynge the blafte
of vaynglorye which he before defyred, now with all
his mynde he began to feke the glory and profytè of
Chryftes chyrche, and fo began he to ordre his condycions
y' from thens forth he myght have ben approved &
thoughe his enemye were his judge.

OF THE FAME OF HIS VERTUE AND
THE RESORTE UNTO HYM THERFORE.

Here upon fhortly the fame of his noble connynge and

excellent vertue bothe ferre & nygh began gloryoufly to
fprynge for which many worthy philofophres (& that
were taken in nombre of the mooft connynge) reforted
bifely unto hym as to a market of good doctryne, fome
for to move queftions and dyfpute, fome (that were of
more godly mynde) to here and to take the holefome
leffons and inftruccyon of good lyvynge : whiche leffons
were fo moche ye more fet by : in how moche they came
from a more noble man and a more wyfe man and hym
alfo whiche had hym felfe fome tyme folowed ye croked
hilles of delycyoufe pleafure. To the faftenynge of good
dyfcyplyne in the myndes of ye herers those thynges feme
to be of grete effecte : whiche be bothe of theyr owne
nature good & alfo be fpoken of fuche a mafter as is
converted to the way of juftyce from the croked & ragged
path of voluptuoufe lyvynge.

THE BURNYNG OF WANTON BOKES.

Fyve bokes that in his youthe of wanton verfis of love
with other lyke fantafies he had made in his vulgar
tongue : all togyther (in deteftacyon of his vyce paffed)
and left thefe tryfles myght be fome evyll occafyon afterwarde, he burned them.

OF HIS STUDY AND DILYGENCE
IN HOLY SCRYPTURE.

From thensforth he gave him felfe day & nyght mooft
fervently to the ftudyes of fcrypture, in whiche he wrote
many noble bokes : whiche well teftyfye bothe his angylyke
wyt, his ardent laboure, and his profounde erudicyon, of
whiche bokes some we have & fome as an ineftimable
treafure we have lofte. Grete lybraries hit is incredible
to confydre with how merveloufe celeryte he red them

over, and wrote out what hym liked : of yᵉ olde fathers of
yᵉ chyrch, fo gret knowlege he had as hit were harde
for hym to have yᵗ hath lyved longe & all his lyfe hath
done nothyng els but red them. Of thefe newer dyvynes
fo good jugement he had yᵗ it myght appere there were
nothynge in ony of them yᵗ were unknowen to him, but
all thynge as rype as though he had all theyr werkes ever
before his eyen, but of all thefe new doctours he fpecyally
commendeth Saynt Thomas⁸ as hym yᵗ enforfeth hym felfe
in a fure piller of truth. He was very quick, wife, & fubtyl
in difpicions & had grete felicite therin while he had yᵗ
hye ftomak. But now a grete while he had bode fuche
conflictes farewell : and every daye more & more hated
them, and fo gretely abhored them that when Hercules
Eftenfis Duke of Ferrare⁹ : fyrft by meffengers and after
by hym felfe : defyred hym to difpute at Ferrare : bycaufe
the generall chapytre of freres prechours was holden
there : longe hit was or he coude be brought therto : but
at the inftant requeft of the Duke whiche very fyngulerly
loved him he came thyder, where he fo behaved hym
felfe yᵗ was wondre to beholde how all yᵉ audyence
rejoyced to here hym, for hit were not poffyble for a man to
utter neyther more connynge nor more connyngely. But hit
was a commune fayenge with hym yᵗ fuche altercacyons
were for a logition and not metely for a phylofophre,
he fayd also that fuche difputacyons gretely profited as
were exercifed with a peafyble mynde to th'enferchynge
of the treuth in fecrete company without grete audyence :
but he fayd that thofe difpicions dyd grete hurte yᵗ were
holden openly to th'oftentacion of lernynge & to wynne
the favoure of the commune people & the commendacyon
of fooles. He thought that utterly hit coulde unneth be but
that with the defyre of worfhyp (whiche thefe gafynge

dyſputers gape after) there is with an inſeparable bonde
annexed the appetite of his confuſyon & rebuke whome
they argue with, whiche appetyte is a dedly wounde to yᵉ
ſoule, & a mortall poyſon to charite.   There was nothing
paſſed hym of thoſe capicions ſoteltes & cavilacions of
ſophyſtrye, nor agayn there was nothyng yᵗ he more
hated & abhored, conſyderyng that they ſerved of nought
but to yᵉ ſhamyng of ſuche other folke as were in very
ſcyence moche better lerned and in thoſe trifles ignoraunt :
and yᵗ unto th'enſercherchynge of yᵉ treuth (to which he
gave contynuall laboure) they profyted lytell or nought.

OF HIS LERNYNGE UNYVERSALLY.

But bycauſe we wyll holde the reder no longer in hande :
we wyll ſpeke of his lernynge but a worde or twayne
generally. Some man hathe ſhyned in eloquence, but ignorance of naturall thynges hathe diſhoneſted hym. Some
man hath floured in the knowledge of dyvers ſtraunge
languages, but he hath wanted all the cognicion of philo-
ſophye. Some man hath redde the invencyons of the
olde philoſophres, but he hath not ben exerciſed in the
new ſcoles. Some man hath ſought connynge as well
philoſophie as dyvinite for prayſe and vayneglorye and
not for ony profyte or encreace of Chryſtes chyrche. But
Pycus all these thynges with equall ſtudy hath ſo receyved
yᵗ they myght ſeme by hepis as a plentyouſe ſtreme to
have flowen in to hym. For he was not of yᵉ condycion
of ſome folke (which to be excellent in one thynge ſet al
other aſyde) but he in all ſciences profyted ſo excellently :
that which of theym ſo ever he had confydered, in him ye
wolde have thought yᵗ he had taken that one for his onely
ſtudye. And all theſe thynges were in hym ſo moche
the more mervelouſe in yᵗ he came therto by hym ſelfe

with yᵉ ſtrength of his owne wytte for the love of God and profyte his chyrche without mayſters, ſo that we may ſaye of hym that Epycure the philoſophre ſayd of hym that he was his owne mayſter.¹⁰

FYVE CAUSES Yᵀ IN SO SHORTE TYME BROUGHT HYM TO SE MERVELOUSE CONNYNGE.

To the bryngynge forth of ſo wondreful effectes in ſo ſmall tyme I conſidre ſyve cauſes to have come togyder: fyrſt an incredyble wyt, ſecondely a merveylouſe faſt memore, thyrdely grete ſubſtaunce by yᵉ which to yᶜ byenge of his bokes as wel laten as greke & other tonges he was eſpecyally holpen. vij.m. ducates he had layde out in the gaderynge to gyther of volumes of all maner of litterature. The fourth cauſe was his beſy and infatigable ſtudy. The fyfte was the contempt diſpyſynge of all erthly thynges.

OF HIS CONDYCYONS AND HIS VERTUE.

But now let us paſſe over thoſe powers of his ſoule which appertayne to underſtondynge & knowledge & let us ſpeke of them yᵗ belonge to yᵉ achevynge of noble actes, let us as we can declare his excellent condicions yᵗ his mynde enflamed to Godwarde may appere, and his riches gyven out to poore folke may be underſtonde, th'entent yᵗ they whiche ſhall heere his vertue may have occaſyon therby to gyve eſpeciall laude & thanke to almyghty God, of whoſe infynyte goodneſſe all grace and vertue cometh.

OF THE SALE OF HIS LORDESHYPPES AND ALMYSSE.

Thre yere before his deth (to th'ende that all the charge

& befynes of rule or lordfhyp fet a fyde he myght lede
his lyfe in reft and peace, wele confyderynge to what ende
this erthely honour & worldly dignite cometh) all his
patrymonye and dominyons : yᵗ is to fay : the thyrde parte
of th'erldome of Mirandula and of Concordia : unto Johan
Francis his nevewe he folde, and that fo good chepe that
hit femed rather a gyft then a fale.¹¹   All that ever he
receyved of this bargayne partly he gave out to poore
folke, partely he beftowed in yᵉ byenge of a lytell londe,
fyndynge of hym & his houfholde.   And over yᵗ : moche
fylver veffell & plate with other precyoufe & coftly uten-
files of howfholde he devyded amonge poore people.   He
was content with meane fare at his table, how be hit fom-
what yet reteynynge of yᵉ olde plenty in deynty vyande
& fylver veffel.   Every daye at certayne houres he gave
hym felfe to prayer.   To pore men alway yf ony came he
plentioufly gave out his money : & not content onely to
gyve that he had hym felf redy : he wrote over yᵗ to one
Hierom Benivenius ¹² a florentin, a well letred man (whom
for his grete love towarde hym & yᵉ integrite of his condycions he fingulerly favored) yᵗ he fholde with his owne
money ever helpe poore folke : & gyve maydens money
to theyre maryage : and alway fende him worde what he
had layde out that he myght paye hit him ageyn.   This
offyce he commytted to hym that he might yᵉ more eafely
by hym as by a faythful meffenger releve yᵉ neceffyte
& miferi of poore nedy people fuche as hym felfe happely
coude not come by yᵉ knowlege of.

OF Yᴱ VOLUNTARY AFFLECCION & PAY-
NING OF HIS OWN BODY.

Over all this : many times (whiche is not to be kepte
fecrete) he gave almes of his owne body : we knowe

many men which (as Saynt Hierom [13] fayth) put forth theyr
hande to poore folke : but with the plefure of yᵉ flesfhe
they be overcomen : but he many days (and namely [14] thofe
dayes whiche reprefent unto us yᵉ paffyon & deth yᵗ
Chryfte fuffred for our fake) bet and fcourged his owne
flefhe in the remembraunce of that grete benefyte and for
clenfynge of his olde offences.

OF HIS PLACABILITE OR BENYGNE NATURE.

He was of chere alwaye mery & of fo benygne nature yᵗ
he was never troubled with angre & he fayd ones to his
nevew that what fo ever fholde happen (fell ther never
fo grete myfadventure) he coude never as hym thought
be moved to wrath but yf his chyftes peryfshed in
whiche his bokes laye yᵗ he had with grete trauayle &
watche compiled : but for as moche as he confydered yᵗ
he laboured onely for yᵉ love of God & profyte of his
chyrche : & yᵗ he had dedicate unto him all his werkes,
his ftudyes & his doynges : & fith he fawe yᵗ fyth God is
almyghty they coulde not mifcarye but yf it were eyther
by his commaundement or by his fufferaunce : he veryly
trufted : fyth God is all good : yᵗ he wolde not fuffre hym
to have that occafion of hevynes. O very happy mynde
which none adverfyte myght oppreffe, which no prof-
peryte might enhaunce : not the connynge of all philo-
fophie was able to make hym proude, not the knowledge of the hebrewe, chaldey & arabie language befyde
greke and laten coulde make hym vayngloryouse, not his
grete fubftaunce, not his noble blode, coulde blowe up his
herte, not yᵉ beauty of his body, not yᵉ grete occafyon of
fynne were able to pull hym bak in to yᵉ voluptuoufe
brode way yᵗ ledeth to helle : what thynge was ther of fo

mervayloufe ftrength y' might overtorne y' mynde of hym: which now (as Seneke fayth) was goten above fortune [15] as he which as well her favoure as her malice hath fet at nought, y' he myght be coupled with a fpiritull knot unto Chryfte and his hevenly cytezeynes.

HOW HE ESCHEWED DYGNITES.

Whan he fawe many men with grete labour & money defyre & byfely purchafe ye offices & dygnites of ye chirche (whiche are now a dayes alas ye whyle communely bought & folde) him felfe refufed to recyve them whan two kynges offred them: whan an other man offred hym grete worldely promocyon yf he wolde go to ye kynges courte: he gave hym fuche an anfwere, that he fholde well knowe that he neyther defyred worfhip ne worldly ryches but rather fet them at nought y' he might ye more quyetly gyve hym felfe to ftudy & ye fervyce of God: this wyfe he perfuaded, y' to a phylofophre and hym y' feketh for wyfedome it was no prayfe to gather rycheffe but to refufe them.

OF THE DISPYSYNGE OF WORLDLY GLORYE.

All prayfe of people and all erthly glorye he reputed utterly for nothyng: but in ye renayeng of this fhadowe of glory he laboured for very glorye which ever more foloweth vertue as an unfeparable fervaunt. He fayd that fame often tymes dyd hurte to men while they lyve, & never good whan they be deed. So moche onely fet he by his lernynge in how moche he knewe that hit was profytable to ye chyrche & to ye extermynation of errours. And over that: he was come to that prycke of perfyte humilite that he lytell forced wyther his workes went out under his owne name or not fo that they might as moche profite as yf they

were gyven oute under his name. And nowe fet he
lytel by ony other bokes fave onely ye bible, in ye onely
ftudi of which he had appoynted hym felfe to fpende
the refedewe of his lyfe, favynge that ye commune profyte
pricked him whan he confydered fo many & fo grete
werkes as he had conceyved & longe travayled upon
howe they were of every man by and by [16] defyred and
loked after.

HOW MOCHE HE SET MORE BY DEVOCYON THAN CONNYNGE.

The lytell affeccyon of an olde man or an olde woman to
Godwarde (were it never fo fmall) he fet more by : then by
all his owne knowlege as well of naturall thynges as
godly. And oftentymes in communicacyon he wolde
admonyfshe his familyar frendes how gretly thefe mortall
thynges bowe and drawe to an ende, howe flyper & how
fallynge hit is y^t we lyve in now : how ferme how ftable
it fhall be y^t we fhal here after lyve in, whether we be
throwen downe in to hell or lyfte up in to heven. Wherfore he exhorted them to turne up theyr myndes to love
God, which was a thynge farre excellynge all the connynge
y^t is poffible for us in this lyfe to obtaine. The fame
thynge alfo in his boke whiche he entytled De Ente et
Uno lyghtfomely he treateth where he interupteth y^e
courfe of his difpicion and turnynge his wordes to Angelus
Politianus (to whom he dedycateth that boke) he wryteth
in this wyfe. But now beholde o my welbeloved Angell
what madnes holdeth us. Love God (while we be in this
body) we rather maye : than eyther knowe him or by
fpeche utter hym. In lovyng him alfo we more profyte
our felfe, we laboure leffe & ferve hym more, & yet had
we lever alwaye by knowlege never fynde y^t thynge that

we feke : then by love to poffede y' thynge whiche alfo
without love were in vayne founde.[17]

OF HIS LIBERALITE & CONTEMPT OF RYCHESSE.

Liberalite onely in hym paffed meafure : for fo ferre was
he from y² begynnyng of ony diligence to erthely thynges
that he femed fom what befprent with the frekyll of
negligence. His frendes oftentymes admonyfhed hym that
he fholde not all utterly difpyce rycheffe, fhewynge hym
y' hit was his difhonefte and rebuke whan it was reported
(were it treue or falfe) that his negligence & fettyng
nought by money gave his fervauntes occafyon of difceyt
& robbry.   Nevertheles that mynde of his (which evermore on hyghe cleved faft in contemplacion & in th'enferchynge of natures counfel) coulde never let downe hit
felfe to y² confideracion and overfeynge of thefe bafe
abjecte and vyle erthly tryfles. His hygh ftuarde came
on a tyme to hym & defyred hym to receyve his accomt
of fuche money as he had in many yeres receyved of
his : and brought forth his bokes of rekenynge. Picus
anfwered hym in this wyfe, my frende (fayth he) I knowe
well ye have mought oftentimes and yet may defceyve
me and ye lyft, wherfore the examinacyon of thefe ex-
penfes fhall not nede. There is no more to do, yf I be
ought in your det I fhall pay you by & by,[18] yf ye be in
myn pay me : eyther now yf ye have hit : or here after yf
ye be now not able.

OF HIS LOVYNGE MYNDE & VERTUOUSE BEHAVOUR TO HIS FRENDES.

His lovers and frendes with grete benygnite & curtefye
he entreted, whom he ufed in all fecrete comminge vertuoufly to exhorte to Godward, whofe goodely wordes fo

effectually wrought in ye herers y^t where a connynge
man (but not fo good as connynge) came to him on a
daye for ye grete fame of his lernyng to commune with
hym, as they fell in talkynge of vertue he was with the
wordes of Picus fo throughly perced that forth with all
he forfoke his accuftomed vyce and reformed his condicyons.   The wordes y^t he fayd unto hym were thefe :
yf we hadde ever more before our eyen ye paynful deth
of Chryft which he fuffred for the love of us : and than
yf we wolde agayne thynke upon our deth : we fholde wele
beware of fynne.   Merveyloufe benignyte & curtefy he
fhewed unto them : not whom ftrength of body or goodes
of fortune magnified but to them whom lernynge & condicions bounde hym to favoure : for fimylytude of maners
is a caufe of love & frendefhyp.   A likenes of condicions
is (as Appollonius fayth) an affinyte.[19]

WHAT HE HATED AND WHAT HE LOVED.

There was nothyng more odioufe nor more intolirable to
hym than as (Horace[20] fayth) ye proud palaces of ftately
lordes : weddynge and worldly befynes he fled almooft a
lyke : notwithftondynge whan he was axed ones in fporte
whyther of thofe two burdeynes femed lyghter & whiche
he wolde chefe yf he fholde of neceffite be dryven to that
one and at his eleccyon : whiche he ftiked thereat a wyle
but at ye laft he fhoke his heed and a lytell fmylyng he
anfwered y^t he had lever take hym to maryage, as y^t
thynge in whiche was leffe fervytude & not fo moche
jeoperdy.   Lyberte above all thynge he loved, to which
both his owne natural affeccon & ye ftudy of phylofophy
enclyned hym : & for y^t was he alwaye wanderyng &
flytynge & wolde never take hym felfe to ony certayne
dwellynge.[21]

OF HIS FERVENT LOVE TO GOD.

Of outward obſervaunces he gave no very grete force : we ſpeke not of thoſe obſervaunces which the chyrche commaundeth to be obſerved, for in thoſe he was dilygent : but we ſpeke of thoſe cerymonyes which folke brynge up ſettynge yᵉ very ſervyce of God a ſyde, which is (as Chryſt ſayth) to be worſhipped in ſpirite & in treuth.   But in the inwarde affectes of the mynde he cleved to God with very fervent love and devocyon : ſome tyme that merveloufe alacrite langwyſshed and almooſt fell, and efte agayne with grete ſtrength roſe up in to God.   In the love of whome he ſo fervently burned that on a tyme as he walked with Johan Frauncis his nevewe in an orcharde at Farrare, in yᵉ talkynge of the love of Chryſt he brake out in to theſe wordes, nevew, ſayd he, this wyll I ſhewe the, I warne the kepe it ſecrete : the ſubſtaunce yᵗ I have lefte after certayne bokes of myne finyſshed I entende to gyve out to pore folke, & fencynge my ſelfe with the crucifyx, bare fote walkynge about the worlde, in every towne and caſtell I purpoſe to preche of Chryſt.   Afterwarde I underſtande by the eſpecyall commaundement of God he chaunged that purpoſe and appoynted to profeſſe hym ſelfe in the ordre of freres prechours.

OF HIS DETH.

In yᵉ yere of our redempcion, M.CCCC.xCiiii. whan he had fulfylled yᵉ xxxii. yere of his age & abode at Florence, he was ſodenly taken with a fervent axes [22] which ſo ferforth crepte in to yᵉ interiori pertes of his body, yᵗ hit dyſpyſed all medycynes & overcame all remedy, and compelled him within thre dayes to ſatisfye nature and repaye her yᵉ lyfe whiche he receyved of her.

OF HIS BEHAVYOUR IN THE EXTREMES OF HIS LYFE.

After that he hadde receyved the holy body of our Savyour whan they offred unto hym the crucyfyx (y[t] in the ymage of Chryftes ineffable paffion fuffred for oure fake he myght ere he gave up the ghoft receyve his full draught of love and compaffyon in the beholdynge of that pytefull figure as a ftronge defence agaynft all adverfyte and a fure port culioufe againft wikked fpirites) the preeft demaunded hym whether he fermly beleved y[t] crucyfyx to be the Image of hym that was very God & very man : whiche in his Godhed was before all time begoten of his father : to whome he is alfo equall in all thynge : and whiche of y[e] Holy Ghoft God alfo : of hym & of the Father coeternalli goynge forth (whiche .iij. per-fones be one God) was in y[e] chafte wombe of our lady a perpetuall virgyne conceyved in time : which fuffred hungre, thruft, hete, colde, laboure, travayle, & watche : and whiche at the lafte for wafshynge of our fpotty fynne contracted and drawen unto us in the fynne of Adame, for the foveraigne love that he had to mankynde, in the aulter of the croffe wyllyngely & gladly fhedde out his mooft precyoufe blode. When y[e] preeft enquyred of him thefe thynges & fuche other as they be wonte to enquere of folke in fuche cafe, Picus anfwered hym y[t] he not onely beleved hit but alfo certaynly knewe it. Whan y[t] one Albertus [23] his fyfters fone : a yonge man both of wit, connynge, & condicyons excellent : began to conforte hym agaynft deth : & by natural reafon to fhewe hym why hit was not to be fered but ftrongely to be taken : as y[t] onely thynge which maketh an ende of all y[e] laboure, payne, trouble, & forowe of this fhort miferable deedly

lyfe : he anfwered y' this was not the cheyefe thyng y'
fholde make hym content to dye : bycaufe y' deth de-
termyneth the manyfolde incommoditees and paynfull
wretchednes of this life : but rather this caufe fholde
make hym not content onely but alfo glad to dye : for
that deth maketh an ende of fynne : in as moche as he
trufted y° fhortnes of his lyfe fholde leve hym no fpace
to fynne and offende.   He afked alfo all his fervauntes
forgyvenes, yf he had ever before that daye offended ony
of them. For whom he had provyded by his teftament viij.
yeres before, for fome of them mete and drynk, for fome
money, eche of them after theyr defervynge. He fhewed
alfo to the above named Albertus & many other credible
perfons y' y° quene of heven came to hym y' nyght with
a mervayloufe fragrant odour refrefshynge all his membres
y' were brofed & frufshed [24] with that fever, & promyfed
him that he fhold not utterly dye. He lay alwaye with
a plefaunt and a mery countenaunce, and in the verye
twytches and panges of deth he fpake as though he
behelde y° hevens opene. And all y' came to hym &
faluted hym offerynge theyr fervyce with very lovyng
wordes he receyved, thanked, & kyffed. The executour
of his moveable goodes he made one Antony his brother.[25]
The heyer of his landes he made y° pore people of the
hofpytall of Florence. And in this wyfe in to y° handes
of oure Savyoure he gave up his fpiryte.

HOW HIS DETH WAS TAKEN.

What forowe and hevynes his departyng out of this
worlde was : both to ryche and pore, hygh & lowe : well
teftyfyeth the prynces of Italye, well wytneffeth the
citees & people, well recordeth the grete benygnyte and
fynguler curtefye of Charles kynge of Fraunce,[26] which as

he came to Florence, entendynge from thens to Rome
and fo forth in his vyage agaynft the Realme of Naples,
herynge of the fykenes of Picus, in all convenyent hafte
he fent hym two of his owne phificions as embaffiatours
both to vifet hym and to do hym all yᵉ helpe they myght:
and over that fent unto hym letters fubfcribed with
his owne hande full of fuche humanyte and courteyfe
offres as the benevolent mynde of fuche a noble prince
and the worthy vertues of Picus required.

OF THE STATE OF HIS SOULE.

After his deth (and not longe after) Hieronimus[27] a frere
prechour of Ferrare, a man as well in connynge as
holynes of lyvynge mooft famous, in a fermone whiche
he reherced in the cheyfe chyrche of all Florence fayd
unto the people in this wyfe. O thou Cyte of Florence
I have a fecrete thynge to fhewe the which is as true as
yᵉ gofpell of Saynt Johan. I wolde have kept hit fecrete
but I am compelled to fhewe hit. For he that hathe
auctoryte to commaunde me, hath byd me publyfshe hit.
I fuppofe veryly that there be none of you but ye knewe
Johan Picus Erle of Mirandula, a man in whom God had
heped many grete gyftes and fynguler graces, yᵉ chyrche
had of hym an ineftymable loffe, for I fuppofe yf he myght
have had the fpace of his lyfe prorogyd: he fholde have
excelled (by fuche workes as he fhold have lefte behynde
hym) all them yᵗ dyed this .viii.C. yere before him. He
was wonte to be converfaunt with me and to breke to
me yᵉ fecretes of his herte: in whiche I perceyved that he
was by privey infpyracion called of God unto relygion.
Wherfore he purpofed oftentymes to obey this infpyra-
cyon and folowe his callynge. Howbehit not beynge
kynde ynoughe for fo grete benefices of God: or called

bak by the tendernes of his flefshe (as he was a man of delicate complexion) he fhranke frome the laboure, or thinkynge happely yᵗ the religion had no nede of hym differred it for a tyme, howbehit this I fpeke onely by conjecture.²⁸ But for this delaye I thretened hym two yere togyther : yᵗ he wolde be punyfshed yf he for-flowthed that purpofe which our Lorde had put in his mynde, & certeynely I prayed to God my felfe (I wyll not lye therfore) that he myght be fom what beten : to compell hym to take that waye whiche God had from above fhewed hym. But I defyred not this fcourge upon hym yᵗ he was beten with : I loked not for that : but oure Lorde hadde fo decreed that he fholde forfake this prefent lyfe and leve a parte of that noble crowne that he fholde have had in heven. Notwithftondyng yᵉ moft benygne juge hath dalt mercyfully with him : and for his plentyoufe almes gyven out with a free and liberall hande unto poore people & for the devout prayers whiche he mooft inftantly offred unto God this favoure he hath : though his foule be not yet in the bofome of oure Lorde in the hevenly joye : yet is hit not on yᵗ other fyde deputed unto perpetual payne, but he is adjuged for a whyle to the fyre of purgatory, there to fuffre payne for a feafon, which I am yᵉ gladder to fhewe you in this by-halfe : to the entent yᵗ they which knewe hym : & fuche infpecially as for his manyfolde benyfyces are fingulerly beholden unto him : fholde now with theyr prayers, almes, & other fuffrages helpe hym. Thefe thynges this holy man Hierom, this fervaunt of God openly affermed, and alfo fayde that he knew wel if he lyed in that place : he were worthy eternall dampnacion. And over yᵗ he fayd yᵗ he had knowen all thofe thinges wythin a certain tyme, but yᵉ wordes which Picus had fayde in his fykenes of ye aperyng of our lady caufed him to doubt & to fere left Picus had ben deceyved by fome illufyon of ye devyll: in as moch as the promyfe of our lady femed to have ben fruftrate by his dethe: but afterward he underftode y^t Picus was deceyved in the equivocacyon of ye worde whyle fhe fpake of ye feconde deth & ever laftyng & he undertoke her of ye fyrft deth & temporall. And after this ye fame Hierom fhewed to his acquayntaunce y^t Picus had after his deth apered unto him all compaced in fire & fhewed unto him y^t he was fuch wife in purgatorye punyfhed for his neglygence & his unkyndnes. Now fyth hit is fo that he is adjuged to y^t fyre from which he fhal undoubtedly depart unto glory & no man is fure how longe hit fhalbe fyrft: & may be ye fhorter tyme for our interceffyons: let every chryften body fhewe theyr charite upon hym to helpe to fpede hym thyder where after the longe habitacion with ye inhabytauntes of this derke worlde (to whom his goodly converfacion gave grete lyght) & after ye darke fyre of purgatory (in whiche venyall offences be clenfed) he may fhortly (yf he be not all redy) entre ye inacceffible & infinite light of heven; where he may in ye prefence of ye foveraygne Godhed fo praye for us y^t we may ye rather by his interceffion be perteyners of y^t infpecable joy which we have prayed to bryng hym fpedely to. Amen. Here endeth ye lyfe of Johan Picus Erle of Mirandula.

Here foloweth thre epiftles of ye fayd Picus: of which thre two be wryten unto Johan Fraunfces his nevew, the thyrde unto one Andrewe Corneus a noble man of Italy.

THE ARGUMENT & MATER OF THE FYRST EPYSTLE OF PICUS UNTO HIS NEVEW JOHAN FRAUNSCES.

Hit apereth by this epiſtle yᵗ Johan Fraunſces the nevew
of Picus had broken his mynde unto Picus and had made
hym of counceyll in ſome ſecrete godly purpoſe whiche he
entended to take upon hym: but what this purpoſe ſholde
be upon this lettre can we not fully perceyve. Nowe
after yᵗ he thus entended, there fell unto hym many
impedimentes & divers occaſyons whiche withſtode his
entent and in maner letted hym & pulled hym bak,
wherfore Picus comforteth hym in this epyſtle and exorteth
hym to perſeveraunce, by ſuch meanes as are in the epyſtle
evydent and playne ynough. Notwithſtondynge in yᵉ
begynnyng of this lettre where he ſayth that the fleſhe
ſhall (but yf we take good hede) make us dronke in the
cuppes of Cerces and myſshappe us in to the lykenes &
fygure of bruyte beeſtes : thoſe wordes yf ye perceyve
theym not be in this wyſe underſtonden. There was
ſomtyme a woman called Circes whiche by enchaunte-
mente as Vyrgyll maketh mencyon uſed with a drynke to
turne as many men as receyved hit in to dyvers likenes
& fygures of ſondrye beeſtes, ſome in to lyones, ſome in
to beeres, ſome in to ſwyne, ſome in to wolfes, which
afterwarde walked ever tame aboute her houſe and wayted
upon her in ſuche uſe or ſervyce as ſhe lyſt to put unto them.
In lykewyſe the fleſshe yf it make us dronke in yᵉ wyne
of voluptuous pleaſure or make the ſoule leve the noble
uſe of his reaſon & enclyne unto ſenſualite and affeccions
of yᵉ body: then the fleſshe chaungeth us from the figure
of reaſonable men in the lykenes of unreaſonable beeſtes,
and yᵗ dyverſly: after the convenience & ſymylytude

betwene our fenfuall affeccyons and the brutyfshe pro-
prytees of fondry beeftes : as the proude harted man in
to a lyon, the irous in to a beere, the lecheroufe in to a
gote, the dronken gloten in to a fwyne, the ravenous
extorcyoner in to a wolfe, the falfe defceyvoure in to a
foxe, mokkynge gefter in to an ape. From which beeftly
fhappe may we never be reftored to our owne lykenes
agayn : unto the tyme we have caft up agayne the drynke
of the bodely affeccyons by which we were in to thefe
fygures enchaunted. Whan there cometh fomtyme a
monftrouse beeft to the towne we ronne and are glad to
paye fome money to have fyght therof, but I fere yf men
wolde loke upon them felfe advyfedly : they fholde fe a
more monftroufe beeft nerer home : for they fholde
perceyve themfelfe by ye wretched inclinacion to divers
beeftly paffyons chaunged in theyr foule not in to the fhap
of one but of many beeftes, y^t is to faye of all them whofe
brutyfh appetytes they folow. Let us then beware as
Picus councelleth us y^t we be not dronken in ye cuppes of
Cerces, y^t is to fay in ye fenfuall affeccions of ye flefsh,
left we deforme ye image of God in our foules, after whofe
image we be made, & make our felfe worfe then idolatres,
for yf he be odioufe to God whiche turneth ye image of a
beeft in to god : how moche is he more odious which
torneth the ymage of God in to a beeft.

JOHAN PICUS ERLE OF MIRANDULA TO JOHAN FRAUNSCES HIS NEVEW BY HIS BROTHER HELTH IN HYM THAT IS VERY HELTH.

That thou hast had many evyll occafyons after thy
departynge which trouble the & ftonde agaynft the vertuoufe purpofe that thou haft taken there is no caufe my

ſone why thou ſholdeſt eyther mervayle therof, be ſory
therfore, or drede hit, but rather how grete a wondre were
this yf onely to yᵉ amonge mortall men yᵉ way laye
open to heven with out ſwet, as though yᵗ now at erſt
the diſceytfull worlde & the curſed devyll ſayled, & as
thoughe thou were not yet in yᵉ fleſshe : which coveyteth
agaynſt the ſpyrite : and which falſe fleſsh (but yf we
watche & loke wel to our ſelf) ſhal make us dronke in yᵉ
cuppes of Circes & ſo deforme us in to monſtrous ſhappes
of brutyſsh & unreaſonable beeſtes.   Remembre alſo that
of theſe evyll occaſyons the holy apoſtle ſaynt James ſayth
thou haſt cauſe to be glad, writynge in this wyſe. Gaudete
fratres quum in temptationes varias incideritis. Be glad
ſayth he my brethren whan ye fall in dyvers temptacions,
and not cauſeles : for what hope is there of glorye yf there
be none hope of victorye : or what place is there for
victory where there is no batayl : he is called to the
crowne & triumphe whiche is provoked to the conflycte &
namely to that conflyct : in which no man may be overcom
againſt his will, & in which we nede none other ſtrength to
vaynquyſsh but yᵗ we lyſt our ſelfe to vaynquiſsh.   Very
happy is a chriſten man ſyth yᵗ yᵉ victory is bothe put in
his owne fre wyll : & the rewarde of the vyctory ſhal be
farre greter than we can eyther hope or wyſshe. Tell me
I pray yᵉ my mooſt dere ſone if ther be ought in this life
of all thoſe thingis : yᵉ delite wherof ſo vexeth and toſſith
theſe erthly myndes. Is ther I ſay oni of thoſe trifles : in
yᵉ geting of which a man muſt not ſuffre many labours
many diſpleaſurs & many miſeries or he get hit.   The
marchaunt thinkith him ſelfe well ſerved if after X yeres
ſailing, after a m. incommoditees, after a m. jeopardyes of
his lyſe he may at laſt have a litle the more gadered to
gyther.   Of the court & ſervyce of this worlde there is

nothyng yᵗ I nede to wryte unto the, the wretchednes wherof the experience hit selfe hath taught the & dayly techeth. In obtaynyng yᵉ favour of yᵉ prynces, in purchafynge the frendfhyp of yᵉ company in ambicyoufe labour for offyces & honoures what an hepe of hevynes there is : how grete anguifsh : how moche befynes & trouble I may rather lerne of the then teche yᵉ, whiche holdyng my felf content with my bokes & refte, of a chylde have lerned to lyve within my degree & as moche as I maye dwellynge with my felfe nothynge out of my felf labour for, or longe for. Now then thefe erthly thynges flyper, uncertayne, vyle & commune alfo to us and bruyte beeft fwetynge & pantynge we fhall unneth obtayne : and loke we than to hevenly thynges & goodly (whiche neyther eye hath feen nor ere hath herde nor herte hath thought) to be drawen flumbry & flepyng magrey our teth : as though neyther God myght reygne nor thofe hevenly citezyns lyve without us. Certaynely if this worldly felicite were goten to us with ydelnes and eafe : than myght fome man that fhrynketh frome labour rather chefe to ferve yᵉ worlde then God. But now yf we be fo labored in the waye of fynne as moche as in the way of God and moche more (wherof the dampned wretches crye out : Laffati fumus in via iniquitatis. We be weryed in the waye of wyckednes) then muft it nedes be a poynte of extreme madnes yf we had not lever labour there where we go from labour to rewarde then where we go from labour to payne. I paffe over how grete peace & felycite hit is to the mynde whan a man hath nothinge that grudgeth his confcience nor is not appaled with the fecrete twiche of ony prevye cryme. This pleafure undoubtedly farre excelleth all yᵉ pleafurs yᵗ in this lyfe may be obteyned or defyred : what thyng is there to be defyred amonge yᵉ delytes of this worlde :

which in yᵉ fekynge wery us, in yᵉ havynge blyndeth us, in yᵉ lefyng payneth us. Doubteſt thou my fone whether the myndes of wycked men be vexed or not with contynuall thought and torment: hit is yᵉ worde of God whiche neyther maye deceyve nor be deceyved. Cor impij quaſi mare fervens quod quiefcere non poteſt. The wycked mannes herte is lyke a ſtormy fee yᵗ maye not reſt, there is to hym nothynge fure, nothyng pefeable, but all thynge ferefull, all thinge forowfull, all thyng deedly. Shall we then envye thefe men: fhall we folow them: & forgetynge our owne countre heven, & our owne hevenly Father where we were free borne: fhall we wylfully make our felfe theyr bondemen: & with them wretchedly lyvyng more wretchedly dye: and at yᵉ laſt mooſt wretchedly in everlaſtyng fyre be punifshed. O the derke myndes of men. O the blynde hertes. Who feyth not more clere than lyght that all thefe thynges be (as they fey) truer than trueth hit felfe, & yet do we not that yᵗ we knowe is to be done. In vayne we wolde pluk our fote out of the clay but we ſtyk ſtyll. There fhall come to the my fone doubte hit not (in thefe places namely where thou art converfaunt) innumerable impedimentes every hour: which myght fere the frome the purpofe of good and vertuoufe lyvynge & (but yf thou be ware) fhall throwe the downe hedlynge. But amonge all thynges the very deedly peſtylence is this: to be converfaunt daye and nyght among them whofe lyfe is not onely on every fyde an allectyve to fynne: but over that all fet in the expugnacion of vertue, under theyr capitayne the devyll, under the banayre of deth, under the ſtipende of hell, fightynge agaynſt heven, agaynſt our Lorde God and agaynſt his Chriſt. But crye thou therfore with yᵉ prophete. Dirumpamus vincula eorum & projiciamus a nobis iugum ipforum.

33

F

Let us breke the bandes of them and let us caſt of the yooke
of them. Theſe be they whom (as yᵉ glorioúſe apoſtle Saynt
Paule ſeith) our Lorde hath delyvered in to the paſſyons of
rebuke and to a reprovable ſenſe to do thoſe thynges that
are not convenyente, full of all iniquite, full of envye, man-
ſlaughter, contencion, gyle, & malice : backbiters, odiouſe to
God, contumelioúſe, proude, ſtately, ſynders of evell thynges,
folyſshe, diſſolute, without affeccion, without covenaunt, without mercy. Whiche whan they dayely ſe the juſtice of God,
yet underſtonde they not yᵗ ſuche as theſe thynges commytte
are worthy deth : not onely they yᵗ do ſuche thynges : but
alſo they which conſent to yᵉ doynge : wherfore my chylde
go thou never aboute to pleaſe them whome vertue diſ-
pleaſeth : but evermore let theſe wordes of yᵉ apoſtyll be
before thyn eyen. Oportet magis Deo placere quàm
hominibus. We muſt rather pleaſe God then men. And
remembre theſe wordes of Saynt Paule alſo. Si hominibus
placerem, ſervus Chriſti non eſſem. If I ſholde pleaſe men
I were not Chriſtes ſervaunt. Let entre in to thyn herte
an holy pryde & have dyſdayne to take them for mayſters
of thy lyvynge whiche have more nede to take yᵉ for a
maiſter of theyrs. Hit were ſarre more ſemynge yᵗ they
ſholde with yᵉ by good lyvynge begyn to be men then
thou ſholdeſt with them by yᵉ levynge of thy good purpoſe
ſhamfully begyn to be a beſt. There holdeth me ſomtyme by almyghty God as hit were even a ſwone and an
inſenſibilite for wondre when I begyn in my ſelfe : I wot
never whether I ſhall ſey : to remembre or to ſorowe, to
mervayle or to bewayle the apetytes of men, or yf I ſhall
more playnly ſpeke : yᵉ very madnes not to beleve the
goſpell whoſe trouthe the blode of marters cryeth, yᵉ
voyce of apoſtles ſowneth, miracles proveth, reaſon con-
ſermeth, yᵉ worlde teſtifyeth, yᵉ elementes ſpeketh,

devylles confeſſeth.   But a ſerre greter madnes is hit yf
thou doubt not but that the goſpell is true: to lyve then as
though thou doubteſt not but that hit were falſe.   For yf
theſe wordes of the wordes of the goſpell be true, that hit
is very harde for a riche man to entre the kyngedome of
heven why do we dayly then gape after the hepynge up of
riches.   And yf this be true that we ſholde ſeke for the
glorye and prayſe not that cometh of men, but that cometh
of God, why do we then ever hange upon the jugement &
opinyon of men and no man rekketh whether God lyke
hym or not.   And yf we ſurely beleve yᵗ ones the tyme
ſhall come in whiche our Lorde ſhall ſaye, go ye curſed
people in to everlaſtynge fyre, & agayne, come ye my
bleſſed chyldren poſſede ye the kyngdome yᵗ hath ben
prepared for you from yᵉ fourmynge of the world, why is
there nothyng then yᵗ we leſſe fere then hell, or yᵗ we leſſe
hope for then the kyngedome of God.   What ſhall we ſay
elles but yᵗ there be many chryſten men in name but ſewe
in dede.   But thou my ſone enforce thy ſelfe to entre
by the ſtreyght gate yᵗ ledeth to heven & take no hede
what thynge many men do : but what thyng yᵉ verey law
of nature, what thyng very reaſon, what thynge our Lorde
hym ſelfe ſheweth yᵉ to be done.   For neyther thy glory ſhal
be leſſe yf thou be happy with ſewe nor thy payne more
eaſy yf thou be wretched with many.   Thou shalt have .ii.
ſpecyally effectuall remedyes agaynſt yᵉ worlde & the
devyll with whiche two as with .ii. whynges thou ſhalt
out of this vale of miſerye be lyfte up in heven, that is to
ſaye, almes dede & prayer.   What maye we do without the
helpe of God, or how ſhall he helpe us yf he be not called
upon.
    But over that : certaynely he ſhall not here the whan
thou calleſt on hym yf thou here not ſyrſt yᵉ pore man

whan he calleth upon yᵉ, and verely hit is accordynge
that God ſholde deſpyſe the beynge a man whan thou
beynge a man deſpyſeſt a man. For hit is wryten : in
what meſure yᵗ ye mete, hit ſhall be mete you agayne.
And in an other place of yᵉ goſpell hit is ſayd: blyſſed be
mercyfull men for they ſhall gete mercy. Whan I ſtyre
the to prayer I ſtyre yᵉ not to yᵉ prayer whiche ſtondeth
in many wordes, but to that prayer whiche in yᵉ ſecrete
chambre of the mynde, in the prevy cloſet of yᵉ ſoule
with very affecte ſpeketh to God, and in yᵉ mooſt lyght-
ſome darkenes of contemplacion not onely preſenteth the
mynde to the Father: but alſo unieth hit with him by
inſpekable wayes which onely they knowe yᵗ have aſſayed.
Nor I care not how longe or how ſhort thy prayer be,
but how effectuall, how ardente, and rather interrupted &
broken betwene with ſighes then drawen on length with
a contynuall rowe & nombre of wordes. Yf thou love
thyne helth, yf thou deſyre to be ſure from yᵉ grennes [29] of
yᵉ devyll, from the ſtormes of this worlde, frome th' awayte
of thyn enemyes, yf thou long to be acceptable to God, yf
thou coveyte to be happy at the laſt : let no day paſſe the
but thou ones at the leſt wiſe preſent thy ſelfe to God by
prayer, and fallyng downe before hym flat to yᵉ grounde
with an humble affecte of devout mynde, not frome yᵉ ex-
tremyte of thy lippes but out of yᵉ inwardnes of thyn herte,
cry theſe wordes of yᵉ prophete. Delicta juventutis mee
& ignorantias meas ne memineris, ſed ſecundum miſericor-
diam tuam memento mei propter bonitatem tuam Domine.
The offences of my youth and myn ignoraunces remembre
not good Lorde, but after thy mercy Lorde for thy goodnes
remembre me. Whan thou ſhalt in thy prayer axe of God:
both yᵉ Holy Spyryte which prayeth for us & eke thyn owne
neceſſyte ſhall every houre put in thy mynde, & alſo

what thou shalte praye for : thou shall fynde mater ynough
in ye redynge of holy scrypture which yt thou woldest
now (settynge poetes fables & trysles a syde) take ever
in thyn hand I hartly pray ye.[30]   Thou mayst do nothynge
more pleasaunte to God, nothynge more profitable to thy
selfe : then yf thyn hande ceafe not day nor nyght to
turne and rede the volumes of holy scrypture.   There
lyeth pryvely in them a certayn hevenly strength quyk
and effectual, wich with a merveylous power transfourmeth
& chaungeth ye reders mynde in to the love of God, yf
they be clene and lowly entreated.   But I have passed
nowe ye boundes of a lettre, ye mater drawynge me forth
& the grete love yt I have had to the, bothe ever before :
& specyally syth yt houre in which I have had fyrst
knowledge of thy moost holy purpose.   Now to make an
ende with this one thynge I warne ye (of which whan we
were last togyther I often talked with ye) that thou never
forget thefe. ii. thynges, yt both ye Sone of God dyed for ye
& yt thou shalt alfo thy selfe dye shortly, lyve thou never
fo longe.   With these twayne as with two spurres, ye one
of fere ye other of love, spurre forthe thyn hors through ye
shorte way of this momentarye lyfe to ye rewarde of
eternall felicyte, syth we neyther ought nor maye prefere
our felfe onye other ende than the endles fruycion of ye
infinite goodnes bothe to foule & body in everlastynge
peace.

Fare well and fere God.[31]

THE MATER OR ARGUMENT OF THE EPISTLE OF PICUS TO ANDEWE CORNEUS.

This Andrewe a worshypfull man and an especiall frende
of Picus hadde by his lettres gyven hym counceyll to

leve the ftudy of phylofophy, as a thynge in which he
thought Picus to have fpent tyme ynough & whiche : but
yf it were applyed to yᵉ ufe of fome actuall befines : he
juged a thyng vayne & unprofytable : wherfore he coun-
ceyled Pycus to furceace of ftudy and put hym felfe with
fome of yᵉ grete prynces of Italy, with whome (as this
Andrew fayd) he fholde be moche more fruytefully
occupyed then alway in the ftudye & lernyng of philo-
fophye, to whom Picus anfwered as in this prefent epeftle
appereth. Where he fayth thefe wordes (By this hit fhold
folowe yᵗ hit were eyther fervyle or at the left wyfe not
pryncely to make yᵉ ftudy of phylofophy other then mercen-
nari) thus he meaneth. Mercennary we cal all thofe thynges
whiche we do for hyre or rewarde. Then he maketh
philofophy mercennary & ufeth hit not as connynge but
as marchaundyfe whiche ftudyeth hit not for pleafure of
hit felfe : or for the inftruccyon of his mynde in mortall
vertue : but to applye hit to fuche thynges where he may
get fome lucre or worldly advauntage.

JOHAN PICUS ERLE OF MYRANDULA TO ANDREWE CORNEUS GRETYNGE.

Ye exhorte me by your letters to the cyvyle and active
lyfe, fayenge yᵗ in vayne : and in maner to my rebuke &
fhame : have I fo longe ftudyed in philofophy : but yf I
wolde at the laft excercife yᵉ lernynge in yᵉ entretynge
of fome profitable actes & outwarde byfynes. Certaynly
my welbeloved Andrewe I had caft awaye bothe coft &
laboure of my ftudy : yf I were fo mynded that I coude
fynde in my herte in this mater to affent unto you &
folowe your councell. This is a very deedly and mon-
ftrous perfuacyon which hath entred the myndes of men :
belevynge that yᵉ ftudyes of phylofophye are of eftates &

prynces : eyther utterly not to be touched : or at left wife
with extreme lyppes to be fypped : and rather to the pompe
& oftentacion of theyr wit then to the culture & profyte
of theyr myndes to be lytel & eafely tafted.   The wordes
of Neoptolemus they holde utterly for a fure decree : that
phylofophy is to be ftudyed eyther never or not longe : [32]
but the fayenges of wyfe men they repute for japes &
very fables : that fure & ftedfaft felicite ftondeth onely in
the goodnes of the mynde, & that thefe outwarde thynges
of y° body or of fortune lytle or nought pertayne unto
us.   But here ye wyll faye to me thus.   I am contente ye
ftudye, but I wolde have you outwardly occupyed alfo.
And I defyre you not fo to embrace Martha that ye fholde
utterly forfake Mary.   Love them & ufe them both, as
well ftudy as worldly occupacion.   Trewly my welbeloved
frende in this poynt I gayne fey you not, they that fo do I
fynde no fault in nor I blame them not, but certaynly hit is
not all one to fey we do well yf we do fo : and to fey we do
evyll but yf we do fo.   This is farre out of the way : to
think that from contemplacyon to the actyfe lyving, that
is to fey from the better to the worfe, is none errour to
declyne : and to thynke that it were fhame to abyde
ftyll in the better and not declyne.   Shall a man then be
rebuked by caufe that he defyryth and enfueth vertue
only for hit felfe : by caufe he ftudyeth y° myfteryes of
God : by caufe he enfercheth the counceyll of nature : by
caufe he ufeth continually this plefaunt eafe & reft :
fekynge none outwarde thyng, difpifing all other thynge :
syth thofe thynges are able fuffyciently to fatisfye y°
defyre of theyr folowers.   By this rekenynge hit is a
thynge eyther fervyle or at y° left wife not princely to
make y° ftudy of wyfdom other then mercennarye : who
may well here this, who may fuffre hit.   Certaynly he

never ftudyed for wyfedome which fo ftudied therfore
that in tyme to come eyther he myght not or wolde not
ftudy therfore, this man rather excercifed y[e] ftudy of
marchaundyfe then of wyfedom. Ye wryte unto me that
hit is tyme for me now to put my felfe in houfhoulde with
fome of the grete prynces of Italy but I fe well y[t] as yet
ye have not knowen the opynion that phylofophres have
of them felfe, which (as Horace fayth) repute them felfe
kynges of kinges:[33] they love lyberte: they can not bere
y[e] proud maners of eftates : they can not ferve. They
dwell with them felfe and be content with the tranquyllyte
of theyr owne mynde, they fuffyce them felfe & more,
they feke nothynge out of them felfe : y[e] thynges that
are had in honoure amonge y[e] commune people : amonge
them be not holden honourable. All that ever the voluptuoufe defyre of men thyrfteth for : or ambycyon fygheth
for : they fet at nought & defpife. Which while hit
belongeth to all men : yet undoubtedly it perteyneth mooft
proprely to them whome fortune hath fo lyberally favoured
that they may lyve not onely well and plenteoufly but alfo
nobly. Thefe grete fortunes lyfte up a man hye and
fett hym out to the fhewe : but oftentymes as a fyerfe
and a fkyttyfsh hors they caft of theyr mayfter. Certeynly
alway they greve and vexe hym and rather tere hym then
bere hym. The golden mediocrite, the meane eftate is to
be defyred whiche fhall bere us as hit were in handes[34] more
eafeli : which fhall obey us & not mayftre us. I therfore abydyng fermely in this opynyon fet more by my
litle houfe, my ftudy, the pleafure of my bokes, y[e] reft and
peace of my mynde : then by all your kynges palaces, all
your commune befynes, all your glory, all the advauntage
that ye hawke after and all the favoure of the court. Nor
I loke not for this fruyte of my ftudy y[t] I may therby

herafter be toffed in the flode and rombelyng of your
worldly befyneffe: but y' I may ones bryng forth the
chyldren that I travayle on: y' I may gyve out fome
bokes of myn owne to the commune proffyte which may
fum what favour yf not of connyng yet at the left wyfe
of wyt and dylygence.   And by caufe ye fhall not thynk
that my travayle & dyligence in ftudy is ony thyng re-
mytted or flakked: I gyve you knowledge y' after grete
fervent labour with moch watch and infatygable travayle
I have lerned both the hebrew language and the chaldey,
and now have I fet hande to overcome the grete dyffyculte
of the araby tonge.   Thefe my dere frende be thynges
whiche to apertaine to a noble prynce I have ever thought
and yet thynke.   Fare ye well.   Wryten at Paris the
.xv. daye of Octobre the yere of grace. M.CCCC.lxxxxii.[35]

THE ARGUMENT OF THE EPYSTLE FOLOWYNGE.

After that Johan Fraunfces ye nevew of Picus had (as hit
apereth in ye fyrft epiftle of Picus to hym) begon a chaunge
in his lyvynge: hit femeth by this lettre y' the company
of the court where he was converfaunt diverfly (as hit is
theyr unmanerly maner) defcanted therof to his rebuke as
them thought: but as trueth was unto theyr owne.   Some
of them juged hit foly, fome called hit hypocrefy, fome
fcorned him, fome fclaundred hym, of all whiche de-
meanour (as we maye of this epiftle conjecture) he wrote
unto this erle Picus his uncle, whiche in this lettre com-
forted & encourageth him, as hit is in ye courfe therof
evydent.

JOHAN PICUS ERLE OF MYRANDULA TO FRAUNSCES HIS NEVEW GRETYNGE IN OUR LORDE.

Happy art thou my fone whan that oure Lorde not onely gyveth the grace wel to lyve but alfo that whyle thou lyveft wel he gyveth ye grace to bere evyl wordes of evyll people for thy lyvynge well. Certaynly as grete a prayfe as hit is to be commended of them y^t are commendable, as grete a commendacion it is to be reproved of them y^t are reprovable. Notwithftondynge my fone I call the not therfor happy by caufe this fals reprofe is worfhypfull & gloryous unto the, but for bycaufe y^t our Lorde Jefu Chryft (which is not onely true but alfo trueth hit felfe) affermeth that oure rewarde fhall be plenteous in heven when men fpeke evyll to us & fpeke all evyll agaynft us lyvynge for his name.[36] This is an Apoftles dignyte : to be reputed dygne afore God to be defamed of wykked folke for his name. For we rede in the gofpell of Luke that the appoftles went joyfull and glad from ye counfeill houfe of the Jewes bycaufe God had accepted theym as worthy to fuffre wronge and repreffe for his fake. Let us therfore joye and be glad yf we be worthy fo grete worfhyp before God y^t his worfhyp be fhewed in our rebuke. And yf we fuffre of ye world ony thyng that is grevous or bytter : let this fwete voyce of our Lorde be our confolacion. Si mundus vos odio habet, fcitote quia priorem me vobis odio habuit. Yf the worlde (fayth our Lorde) hate you, knowe ye y^t hit hated me before you. If ye worlde then hated him by whome ye worlde was made : we mooft vyle & fimple men and worthy (yf we confydre our wreched lyvynge well) all fhame & reproufe : yf folke bakbyte us & faye evyll of us : ſhall we ſo grevouſly take hit yᵗ leſt they ſhold ſay evyll we ſholde begyn to do evyll. Let us rather gladly receyve theſe evyl wordes, and yf we be not ſo happy to ſuffre for vertue & trueth as the olde ſeyntes ſuffred betynges, byndynges, pryſon, ſwerdes, & deth : let us thynke at the leſt wiſe we be well ſerved yf we have yᵉ grace to ſuffre chydynge, detraccion, & hatred of wikked men, leſt yᵗ yf all occaſion of deſervynge be taken awaye ther be leſte us none hope of rewarde. Yf men for thy good lyvynge prayſe the : thy vertue certaynly in yᵗ hit is vertue maketh the lyke unto Chryſt : but in that hit is prayſed hit maketh the unlike him : which for the reward of his vertue receyved yᵉ opprobryouſe deth of the croſſe : for which as the apoſtle ſayth God hath exalted hym and gyven hym a name yᵗ is above all names. More deſyrefull is than to be condempned of the worlde and exalted of God then to be exalted of the worlde and condempned of God : yᵉ worlde condemneth to lyfe, God exalteth to glorye : yᵉ worlde exalteth to a fall, God condempneth to yᵉ fyre of hell. Fynaly yf yᵉ worlde ſawne upon yᵉ : unneth hit may be but yᵗ thy vertue (which all lyfte upwarde ſholde have God alone to pleaſe) ſhall ſomwhat unto yᵉ blandiſshynge of yᵉ worlde & favoure of yᵉ people inclyne. And ſo thoughe hit leſe nothynge of yᵉ integrite of our perſeccion : yet hit leſeth of the rewarde, which reward whyle hit begynneth to be payde in yᵉ worlde where all thynge is lytle, hit ſhal be leſſe in heven where al thing is grete. O happy rebukes which make us ſure : yᵗ neither yᵉ floure of our vertue ſhall wyther with the peſtilent blaſt of vaynglorye : nor our eternall rewarde be mynyſshed for the vayn promocion of a lytell populare fame. Let us my ſone love theſe rebukes, & onely of yᵉ ignomynye and repreſe of our Lordes croſſe

let us lyke feythfull fervauntes with an holy ambycyon
be proude. We (fayth Saynt Paule) preche Chryft cruci-
fyed, which is unto y\u1d49 Jewes difpite, unto y\u1d49 Gentyles foly,
unto us y\u1d49 vertue and wyfedom of God. The wyfdom of
this worlde is folyfshnes afore God, & the foly of Chryft is
y\u1d57 by which he hath overcome y\u1d49 wyfedom of y\u1d49 worlde:
by whiche hit hath pleafed God to make his belivyng
people fafe.

If that thou doubte not but y\u1d57 they be madde whiche
bakbite thy vertue: which the chryften lyvynge y\u1d57 is
very wifedom reputeth for madnes: confidre than how
moche were thy madnes, yf thou fholdeft for the jugement of madde men fwarve frome the good inftitution of
thy lyfe, namely fith all errour is with amendement to be
taken awaye & not with imitacion & folowynge to be
encreafed. Let theym therfore nyghe, let theym bawl,
let them barke, go thou boldely forth thy journey as
thou haft begone, and of the wyckednes & myfery confidre
how moche thy felfe arte beholden to God: whiche hath
illumined y\u1d49 fyttynge in the fhadowe of dethe, and tranf-
latynge the out of the company of them (which lyke
dronken men with out a guyde wandre hyther and
thyther in obfcure derkenes) hath affociate the to the
chyldren of lyght. Let that fame fwete voyce of our
Lorde alwaye fowne in thyn eres. Sine mortuos fepelire
mortuos fuos, tu me fequere. Let deed men alone with
deed men, folowe thou me. Deed be they that lyve not to
God, and in the fpace of this temporall dethe laboryoufly
purchafe them felfe eternall deth. Of whom yf you axe
wherto they drawe: wherto they referre theyr ftudyes,
theyr werkes & theyr befynes, & fynally what ende they
have appoynted them felfe in the adepcyon wherof they
fholde be happy: eyther they fhall have utterly nothynge

to anfwere, or they fhall bryng forth wordes repugnaunt
in them felf & contrary eche to other lyke the ravynge of
bedelem people. Nor they wot never them felfe what
they do, but lyke them that fwyme in fwyfte flodes they
be borne forth with yᵉ violence of evyll cuftom as hit were
with the boyftious courfe of yᵉ ftreme. And theyr wik-
kednes blyndynge them on this fyde : & the devyl prik-
kynge them forwarde on that fyde : they renne forthe
hedlyng in to all mifchiefe, as blynde guydes of blynde
men, tyll that dethe fet on them unware, & tyll that hit
be fayd unto them that Chryft fayth in the gofpell, my
frende this nyght yᵉ devylles fhall take thy foule from
the : thefe goodes then that thou hafte gedered whofe
fhall they be. Then fhall they envy them whom they
defpifed. Then fhal they commend them that they
mokked. Then fhall they coveyte to enfew them in lyvyng
whan they may not : whom whan they myght have en-
fewed they purfewed. Stop therfore thyn eres my mooft
dere fone, & what fo ever men fey of yᵉ, what fo ever men
thynke on yᵉ, accompt hit for nothynge, but regarde onely
yᵉ jugement of God, which fhall yelde every man after
his owne werkes when he fhall fhewe hym felfe frome
heven with yᵉ aungels of his vertue : in flame of fyre
doynge vengeaunce upon them that have not knowen
God nor obeyed his gofpell, wich (as the apoftle feyth)
fhal fuffre in deth eternall peyn, from yᵉ face of our
Lorde, & frome the glory of his vertue, whan he fhall come
to be gloryed of his feyntes & to be made merveylous in
all them yᵗ have beleved. Hit is wryten. Nolite timere
qui corpus poffunt occidere, fed qui animam poteft mittere
in gehennam. Fere not them (feyth our Lorde) that may
fle the body : but fere hym yᵗ may caft the foule in to
helle. How moche leffe then be they to be fered : yᵗ

may neyther hurt foule nor body : which yf they now bakbyte yᵉ lyvynge vertuoufly, they fhall do the fame never the
leffe : yf (vertue forfaken) thou were over whelmed with
vyce : not for yᵗ vyce difpleafeth them but for yᵗ yᵉ vyce
of bakbytynge alway pleafeth them. Flee yf thou love
thyn helth, flee as ferre as thou mayft theyr companye,
and retournynge to thy felfe oftentymes fecretly pray
unto yᵉ mooft benygne father of heven, cryenge with the
prophete. Ad Te Domine levaui animam meam : Deus
meus in Te confido, non erubefcam, etiam fi irrideant me
inimici mei. Etenim univerfi qui fperant in Te non confundentur. Confundantur iniqua agentes fupervacue.
Vias tuas Domine demonftra mihi, et femitas tuas edoce
me. Dirige me in veritate tua, et doce me : quia Tu es
Deus Salvator meus, et in Te fperabo tota die.[37] That is to
faye. To Yᵉ Lorde I lyfte up my foule: in The I truft, I fhall
not be fhamed, & thoughe myne enemies mok me. Certaynly all they yᵗ truft in The fhall not be a fhamed. Let
them be a fhamed that worke wyckednes in vayne. Thy
weyes good Lorde fhewe me, and thy pathes teche me.
Directe me in thy trueth, and teche me : for thou arte God
my Savyoure, in The fhall I truft all the daye. Remembre
alfo my fone yᵗ the dethe lyeth at hande. Remembre
that all the tyme of our lyfe is but a moment & yet leffe
than a moment. Remembre how curfed our olde enemy
is : whiche offereth us yᵉ kyngdomes of this world that he
myght beryve us yᵉ kyngdome of heven : how falfe the
flefshly plefures : which therefore embrace us yᵗ they
might ftrangle us : how difceyteful thefe worldly
honoures : which therfore lyfte us up : yᵗ they myght
throwe us downe : how deedly these rycheffes : whiche
the more they fede us, yᵉ more they poyfon us : how
fhorte, how uncertayne, how fhadowe like falfe ymaginary

hit is y* all thefe thynges togyther may brynge us : &
though they flowe to us as we wolde wyfsh them.
Remembre agayne how grete thynges be promyfed and
prepared for them : which difpifynge thefe prefent thynges
defire and longe for that countre whofe kynge is yᵉ God-
heed, whofe law is charite, whofe mefure is eternite.
Occupi thy mynde with thefe meditacyons and fuche
other yᵗ may waken the when thou flepeft, kyndle yᵉ
when thou waxes colde, conferme the when thou wavereft,
& exhibit yᵉ whynges of the love of God whyle thou
laboreft to hevenwarde, that whan thou comeft home to
us (which with grete defyre we loke for) we may fe not
onely hym that we coveyte but alfo fuche a maner one
as we coveyte.   Fare well and love God whom of olde
thou haft begon to fere.   At Ferare the. ii. day of July
the yere of our redempcion.   M.CCCC.lxxxxii.

THE INTERPRETACION OF JOHAN PICUS UPON THIS PSALME CONSERVA ME DOMINE.[38]

Conferva me Domine quoniam fperavi in Te.   Dixi
Domino : Deus meus es Tu, quoniam bonorum meorum
non eges.   Sanctis qui funt in terra mirificavit voluntates
fuas.   Multiplicate funt infirmitates eorum poftea acceleraverunt.   Non congregabo conventicula eorum de fanguinibus : nec memor ero nominum eorum per labia mea.
Dominus pars hereditatis mee & calicis mei : Tu es qui
reftitues hereditatem meam mihi.   Funes ceciderunt mihi
in preclaris : etenim hereditas mea preclara eft mihi.
Benedicam Dominum qui tribuit mihi intellectum : et
vfque ad noctem increpuerunt me renes mei.   Providebam
Deum in confpectu meo femper, quoniam a dextris
eft mihi ne commovear.   Propter hoc letatum eft

cor meum et exultavit lingua mea infuper et caro mea requiefcet in fpe. Quia non derelinques animam meam in inferno : nec dabis fanctum tuum videre corruptionem. Notas mihi fecifti vias vite : adimplebis me letitia cum vultu tuo. Delectationes in dextera tua vfque in finem.

Conferva me Domine. Kepe me good Lorde. If ony perfyte man loke upon his owne eftate there is one parell therin, y' is to wyte, left he wax proude of his vertue, and therfore Davyd fpekyng in y' perfon of a ryghteous man of his eftate begynneth with thefe wordes. Conferva me Domine. That is to faye, kepe me good Lorde : whiche worde kepe me : yf it be well confydered : taketh awaye all occafyon of pryde. For he that is able of hym felf ony thynge to gete is able of him felf that fame thynge to kepe. He that afketh then of God to be kepte in the ftate of vertue fignifyeth in that afkynge that from the begynnynge he gote not that vertue by hym felfe. He then whiche remembreth y' he attayned his vertue : not by his owne power but by the power of God : may not be proude therof but rather humbled before God after thofe wordes of th apoftle. Quid habes quod non accepifti. What haft thou that thou haft not receyved. And yf thou haft receyved hit : why arte thou proude therof as though thou haddeft not receyved it. Two wordes then be there which we fholde ever have in our mouthe : y' one. Miferere mei Deus. Have mercy on me Lorde : whan we remembre our vyce : that other. Conferva me Deus. Kepe me good Lorde : when we remembre our vertue.

Quoniam fperavi in Te. For I have trufted in Y'. This one thynge is it that maketh us obtayne of God oure petycion, y' is to wyte, whan we have a full hope & truft that we fhall fpede. Yf we obferve thefe two thynges in our requeſtes, yᵗ is to wyte, yᵗ we requyre nothynge but that whiche is good for us and yᵗ we requyre hit ardently with a ſure hope that God ſhall here us, our prayers ſhall never be voide. Wherfore whan we miſſe the effecte of our petycyon, eyther hit is for yᵗ we aſke ſuch thynge as is noyous unto us, for (as Chriſt ſayth) we wot never what we aſke, and Jeſus ſayd what ſo ever ye ſhall aſke in my name hit ſhall be gyven you (this name Jeſus ſignifyeth a ſavyour, and therfore there is nothynge aſked in yᵉ name of Jeſus but that is holſome and helpyng to the ſalvacion of the aſker) or elles God hereth not oure prayoure by-cauſe that thoughe yᵉ thynge yᵗ we requyre be good yet we aſke hit not well, for we aſke hit with lytle hope. And he yᵗ aſketh doubtyngely aſketh coldely & therfore Saynt James biddeth us aſke in ſayth nothyng doubtyng.

Dixi Domino: Deus meus es Tu. I have ſayd to our Lorde: my God arte Thou. After that he hath warded & fenced him ſelfe agaynſt pryd he deſcrybeth in theſe wordes his eſtate. All the eſtate of a ryghteous man ſtandeth in theſe wordes. Dixi Domino: Deus meus es Tu. I have ſayd to oure Lorde: my God arte Thou. Whiche wordes though they ſeme commune to all folke, yet are there very few yᵗ may ſaye them truely. That thyng a man taketh for his god that he taketh for his chyefe good. And that thynge taketh he for his chyefe good which onely had, though all other thynges lak, he thynketh hym ſelfe happy, & whiche onely lakyng, though he have al other thynges, he thinketh him ſelf unhappy. The negard then ſeyth to his money: deus meus es tu, my god art thou. For though honour fayle & helth and ſtrenghte and frendes, ſo he have money he thynketh him ſelfe well. And yf he have al thoſe thinges yᵗ we have ſpoken of, yf money fayle he thinketh him ſelfe unhappy. The gloton ſeyth unto his fleſshly luſt, yᵉ ambyciouſe man ſeyth to his vaynglory: my god art thou. Se than how ſew may trewly ſey theſe wordes, I have ſayde to oure Lorde: my God arte Thou. For onely he maye trewly ſaye it whiche is content with God alone: ſo yᵗ yf there were offred hym all the kyngdomes of the worlde and all the good that is in erth and all the good that is in heven, he wolde not ones offende God to have them all. In theſe wordes than, I have ſeyd to our Lord: my God art Thou, ſtandeth all the ſtate of a ryght wyſe man.

Quoniam bonorum meorum non eges. For thou haſt no nede of my good. In theſe wordes he ſheweth yᵉ cauſe why he ſayth onely to our Lorde: Deus meus es tu, my God art Thou. The cauſe is for that onely oure Lorde hath no nede of oure good. There is no creature but yᵗ it nedeth other creatures, and though they be of leſſe perfeccyon than hit ſelfe, as phyloſophers and divynes proven: for yf theſe more imperfyte creatures were not, yᵉ other that are more parſyte coude not be. For yf ony parte of yᵉ hole unyverſyte of creatures were diſtroyed & fallen to nought all the hole were ſubverted. For cer-taynly one part of that univerſyte periſshyng all parties periſsh, and all creatures be partis of yᵗ univerſyte, of which univerſyte God is no parte, but he is the begynnyng nothyng there upon dependynge. For nothynge truely wanne he by yᵉ creacyon of this worlde, nor nothynge ſholde he leſe yf the worlde were adnychylate and turned to nought agayn. Than onely God is he whiche hath no nede of oure good. Well ought we certaynly to be a ſhamed to take ſuche thynge for god as hath nede of us, & ſuche is every creature. Moreover we ſhold not accept for god, yᵗ is to ſaye for the chyeſe goodnes, but onely yᵗ thynge whiche is the mooſt foverayne goodnes of all thynges, and that is not the goodnes of ony creature, onely therfore to our Lorde ought we to faye : my God art Thou.

Sanctis qui funt in terra ejus mirificavit voluntates fuas. To his fayntes that are in ye londe of hym he hath made mervelous his willes. After God fholde we fpecially love them which are nereft joyned unto God, as be the holy aungelles & blyffed fayntes that are in theyr countree of heven : therfore after that he had fayd to oure Lorde : my God arte thou : he addeth ther-unto that oure Lorde hathe made mervelous his wylles, y^t is to faye he hathe made mervelous his loves and his defyres towarde his feyntes that are in the londe of hym, that is to wyte, in the countree of heven whiche is called ye londe of God and the londe of lyvynge people. And veryly yf we inwardly confydre how grete is the felicite of that countree & how moche is ye mifery of this worlde, how grete is ye goodnes and charyte of thofe bleffed citezyns : we fhall continually defyre to be hens that we were there. Thefe thynges & fuch other whan we remembre, we fhold ever more take hede y^t our medi-tacions be not unfruytfull, but that of every meditacyon we fhold alwayes purchase one vertue or other, as for enfample by this meditacyon of the goodnes of that hevenly countree we fholde wynne this vertue that we fholde not onely ftrongly fuffre deth and pacyently whan our tyme cometh or yf hit were put unto us for ye faith of Chryft : but alfo we fholde wyllyngely and gladly longe therfore, defyrynge to be departed out of this vale of wretchydnes y^t we may reygne in y^t hevenly countree with God & his holy fayntes.

Multiplicate funt infirmitates eorum poftea accelera-verunt. Theyr infyrmytees be multyplyed and after they hafted. Thefe wordes the prophete fpeketh of wycked men. By infyrmytees he underftondeth idoles and fo hit is in y° hebrew text. For as good folke have but one God whom they worfhyp, fo evyll folke have many goddes and idoles, for they have many voluptuoufe pleafures many vayne defyres many dyvers paffyons whiche they ferve, & wherfore feke they many fondry pleafures? certainly for bycaufe they can fynde none y' can fet theyr herte at reft & for y' (as y° prophete fayth) wycked men walk about in a circuet or compace wherof there is none ende. Now after thefe wordes: theyr Idoles be multiplied: hit foloweth. After they hafted: y' is to fay: after theyr Idoles, after theyr paffyons and beeftly defyres they ronne forth hedlynge unadvyfedly without ony confideracyon. And in this be we taught that we fholde as fpedely ronne to vertue as they ronne to vyce, & y' we fhold with no leffe dylygence ferve our Lorde God than they ferve theyr lorde y° devyll. The juft man confyderyng y° eftate of evyll folke determineth fermly with hym felfe (as we fholde alfo) that utterly he wyll in no wyfe folowe them, & therfore he faith. Non congregabo conventicula eorum de fanguinibus: nec memor ero nominum. I fhall not gather the congregacyon of them frome the blode: nor I fhall not remembre theyr names, he fayth, from the blode: both bycaufe Idolatres were wont to gather the blode of theyr facrefyce togyther and theraboute to do theyr ferymonyes: and alfo for that all the lyfes of evyll men forfaken reafon whiche ftondeth all in the foule, and folowen fenfualyte that ftondeth all in y° blode, the prophete faith not onely that he wyll not gather theyr congregacyon togyther from y° blode, that is to fay y' he wolde do no facrefyce to thofe idoles but alfo that he wolde not remembre theyr names,

that is to say that he wolde not talke nor speke of y^e
voluptuouse delytes whiche are evyll peoples goddes,
which we myght yet lawfully do: shewynge us by y^t:
that a parfyte man sholde abstayne not onely from unlawfull
pleasures but also frome lawfull, to th'ende y^t he may all
togyther hole have his mynde in to hevenwarde and the
more purely entende unto the contemplacion of hevenly
thynges. And for as moche as some man wolde peradventure thynke y^t hit were soly for a man utterly to de-
pryve him selfe from all pleasures, therfor ye prophete
addeth. Dominus pars hereditatis mee. Our Lorde is
ye part of myn enheretaunce. As though he wolde saye.
Mervayle the not though I forsake all thynge to th'entent
y^t I may have ye possessyon of God in whom all other
thynges also be possessed. This shold be the voyce of
every good chrysten man. Dominus pars hereditatis mee.
God is the parte of myne enheretaunce. For certaynly
we chrysten people to whom God is promysed for an
enheretaunce ought to be ashamed to desyre ony thyng
besyde hym. But for y^t some man myght happely repute
hit for a grete presumpcion y^t a man sholde promyse
hymselfe God for his enherytaunce, therfore ye prophete
putteth therto. Tu es qui restitues hereditatem meam
michi. Thou good Lorde arte he that shall restore myne
enherytaunce unto me. As though he wolde saye. O
good Lorde my God I know well that I am nothynge in
respect of Y^e, I wote well I am unable to assende by myne
owne strength so hyghe to have Y^e in possessyon, but Thou
arte he y^t shalt drawe me to the by thy grace, Thou arte he
that shalte gyve thy selfe in possession unto me. Let a
ryghteous man then consydre how grete a felicite hit is to
have God fall unto hym as his enherytaunce: hit foloweth
in the psalme. Funes ceciderunt mihi in preclaris. The

cordes have fallen to me nobly. The partes and lottes of enherytaunces were of olde tyme met out and dyvyded by cordes or ropes. Thefe wordes then, the ropes or cordes have fallen to me nobly, be as moche to fay as the parte or lot of myne enherytaunce is noble. But for as moche as there be many men which though they be called to this grete felycite (as indede all chriften people are) yet they fet lytel thereby and often tymes chaunge hit for a fmall fymple delyte, therfore yᵉ prophete faith fuyngly. Hereditas mea preclara eft michi. Myn enheritaunce is noble to me. As though he wolde fay that as hit is noble in hit felfe fo hit is noble to me, that is to faye I reputed hit noble, and all other thynges in refpecte of hit I repute (as Saynt Paule fayth) for donge. But for as moche as to have this lyght of underftandynge whereby a man may know this gyft that is gyven hym of God to be the gyft of God, therfore the prophete fuyngely fayth. Benedicam Dominum, qui tribuit intellectum. That is to faye. I fhall blyffe our Lorde which hath gyven me underftondinge. But in fo moche as a man oftentymes entendeth after reafon to ferve God, and yᵗ notwithftondyng yet fenfualite and the flefsh repugneth : than is a man perfyte whan yᵗ not his foule onely but alfo his flefsh drawe forthe to Godwarde after thofe wordes of the prophete in an other pfalme. Cor meum & caro mea exultaverunt in Deum vivum. That is to faye. My mynde & my flefshe both have joyed in to livynge God. And for this the prophete fayth here fuyngely. Et ufque ad noctem increpuerunt me renes mei. My reynes or kidney hath chyden me unto the nyght. That is to faye. My reynes, in which is wont to be the greteft inclinacyon to concupifcence, not onely nowe enclyne me not to fynne but alfo chydeth me, that is to fay, withdrawe me from fynne unto the nyght, that is to faye,

they fo ferforth withdraw me from fynne that wyllyngly
they afflyct and payne my body.   Afflyccyon is in fcrypture oftentymes fignified by the nyght bycaufe hit is the
mooft dyfcomfortable feafon.   Then fuyngly the prophete
fheweth what is y° rote of this privacion or takynge awaye
of flefshly concupifcence in a man, fayenge.   Providebam
Deum in confpectu meo femper.   I provyded God alway
before me fight.   For yf a man had God alwaye before his
eyen as a ruler of all his werkes, & in all his werkes he
fholde neyther feke his owne lucre his glorye nor his
owne pleafure but onely to y° pleafure of God, he fhold
fhortly be perfyte.   And for as moche as he y° fo dooth
profpereth in al thynge, therfore it foloweth.   Ipfe a
dextris eft mihi ne commovear.   He is on my ryght hand
that I be not moved or troubled.   Then the prophete
declareth how grete is y° felycite of a juft man, whiche
fhall be everlaftyngly blyffed bothe in body and in foule,
and therfore he fayth.   Letatum eft cor meum.   My foule
is glad knowyng y° after deth heven is made redy for hym.
Et caro mea requiefcet in fpe.   And my flefshe fhall reft in
hope.   That is to faye that thoughe it joye not by and by as
in receyvynge his gloryous eftate medyatly after the deth,[39]
yet hit refteth in the fepulcre with this hope that it fhall
aryfe in the daye of judgemente immortall and fhynynge
with his foule.   And alfo the prophete more expreffely
declareth in the verfe folowing.   For where he fayd thus,
my foule is glad, he addeth the caufe, fayenge.   Quia non
derelinques animam meam in inferno.   For thou fhalt not
leve my foule in hell.   Alfo where the prophete fayd that
his flefsh fholde reft in hope he fheweth the caufe, fayeng.
Nec dabis fanctum tuum videre corruptionem.   Nor thou
fhalte not fuffre thy faynt to fe corrupcyon, that is to faye,
thou fhalte not fuffre y° flefshe of a good man to be cor-

rupted. For that that was corruptyble shall aryse incorruptible. And for as moche as Chryst was the fyrst whiche entred paradise and opened the lyfe unto us, and was the fyrst that rose agayne and the cause of our resurreccyon : therefore these wordes that we have spoken of the resurreccyon ben pryncipally understonden of Christ, as Saynt Peter ye apostle hath declared, & secondaryly they may be understonden of us in y^t we be the membres of Christ, which onely never sawe corrupcyon, for his holy body was in his sepulcre nothyng putrified. For as moche then as ye way of good lyvyng bryngeth us to a perpetuall lyfe of soule & body, therfore ye prophete sayth. Notas mihi fecisti vias vite. Thou hast made the wayes of lyfe knowen unto me. And bycause that all the felycite of that stondeth in the clere beholdynge and fruycion of God, therfore hit foloweth. Adimplebis me letitia cum vultu tuo. Thou shalt fyll me full of gladnes with thy chere. And for that our felicite shall be everlastynge, therfore he sayth. Delectationes in dextra tua usque in finem. Delectacion & joy shall be on thy ryght hande for ever : he sayth on thy ryght hand bycause y^t our felycite is fulfylled in the vysyon and fruytion of the humanyte of Chryst which sytteth in heven on ye ryght hande of his father's majeste, after ye wordes of Saint Johan. Hec est tota merces, vt videamus Deum, & quem misisti Jesum Christum. That is all oure rewarde that we maye beholde God and Jesus Chryst whome thou hast sent : to whiche rewarde he brynge us that sytteth there and prayeth for us. Amen.

HERE BEGYN .XII. RULES OF JOHAN PICUS ERLE OF MYRANDULA PARTELY EXCYTYNG PARTELY DYRECTYNGE A MAN IN SPYRYTUALL BATAYLE.[40]

Who ſo to vertue eſtemeth the waye
Bycauſe we muſt have warre contynuall
Agaynſt yᵉ worlde, yᵉ fleſsh, yᵉ devyll, that aye
Enforce them ſelfe to make us bonde & thrall,
Let hym remembre that cheſe what way he ſhall
Even after the worlde, yet muſt he nede ſuſteyn
Sorow, adverſite, labour, greyfe, and payne.

THE SECONDE RULE.

Thynke in this wretched worldes beſy woo
The batayll more ſharpe & lenger is I wys
With more laboure and leſſe fruyte alſo
In whiche the ende of laboure labour is :
And when the worlde hath left us after this
Voyde of all vertue : the rewarde when we dye
Is nought but fyre and payne perpetually.

THE THYRDE RULE.

Conſydre well that ſoly it is and vayne
To loke for heven with pleaſure and delyght.
Sith Chryſt our Lorde and ſovereyne captayne
Aſcended never but by manly fyght
And bytter paſſion, then were it no ryght
That ony ſervaunt, ye wyll your ſelfe recorde,
Sholde ſtonde in better condicyon than his lorde.

THE FOURTH RULE.

Thynke how that we not onely fholde not grudge
But eke be glad and joyfull of this fyght,
And longe therfore all though we coude not judge
How that therby redounde unto us myght
Ony profyte, but onely for delyght
To be confourmed and lyke in fome behavour
To Jefu Chryft our bleffed Lorde & Savyoure.

As often as thou doft warre and ftryve,
By the refyftence of ony fynfull mocyon,
Agaynft ony of thy fenfuall wyttes fyve,
Caft in thy minde as oft with good devocyon
How thou refembleft Chryft : as with fowre pocyon
If thou payne thy taft : remembre therewithall
How Chryft for the tafted eyfell[41] and gall.

Yf thou withdrawe thyn handes and forbere
The raven of ony thynge : remembre than
How his innocent handes nayled were.
Yf thou be tempte with pryde : thynke how that whan
He was in forme of God : yet of a bonde man
He toke the fhap and humbled hym felfe for the
To the mooft odioufe and vyle deth of a tree.

Confydre when thou arte moved to be wrothe
He who that was God, and of all men the beft,
Seynge hym felfe fcorned, fcorged both,
And as a thefe betwene .ii. theves threft
With all rebuke and fhame : yet from his breft
Came never figne of wrath or of difdayne,
But pacyently endured all the payne.

Thus every ſnare and engyne of the devyll
Yf thou this wyſe peruſe them by and by :
There can be none ſo curſed or ſo evyll
But to ſome vertue thou mayſt it applye.
For ofte thou ſhalt : refyſtyng valyauntly
The ſendes myght and ſotle fyery darte :
Our Savyour Cryſt reſemble in ſome parte.

THE FYFT RULE.

Remembre well that we in no wyſe muſt
Neyther in the foreſayd eſpyrytuell armoure
Nor ony other remedy put our truſt,
But onely in the vertue ſtrength of our Savyour :
For he it is by whoſe myghty powre
The worlde was veynquyſshed & his prynce caſt out :
Whiche reygned before in all the erthe about.

In hym let us truſt to overcome all evyll,
In hym let us put our hope and confydence,
To ſubdewe the ſleſshe and maſter yᵉ devyll,
To hym be all honour and lowly reverence :
Oft ſholde we requyre with all our dylygence
With prayer, with teeres, & lamentable playntes
The ayde of his grace and his holy ſayntes.

THE SYXTE RULE.

One ſynne vaynquyſshed loke thou not tarye,
But lye in awayte for another every houre,
For as a wood⁴² lyon the ſende our adverſarye
Rynneth aboute ſekynge whom he may devoure :
Wherfore contynually upon thy towre,
Leſt he the unpurveyed and unredy catche,
Thou muſt with the prophete ſtonde & kepe watche.

THE .VII. RULE.

Enforce thy felfe not onely for to ftonde
Unvaynquyfshed agaynft the devyls myght,
But over that take valyauntly on hande
To vaynquyfshe hym and put hym unto flyght :
And that is whan of y° fame dede thought or fyght
By whych he wolde have the with fynne contract
Thou takeft occafyon of fome good vertuoufe acte.

Some tyme he fecretly caftyth in thy mynde
Some lawdable dede to ftere the to to pryde,
As vayn glorye makyth many a man blynde.
But let humylite be thy fure guyde,
Thy good wark to God let hit be applyede,
Thynke hit not thyn but a gyft of his
Of whofe grace undowtedly all goodnes is.

THE .VIII. RULE.

The tyme of batayle fo put thy felfe in preace[43]
As though thou fhuldeft after that victorye
Enjoye for ever a perpetuall peace :
For God of his goodnes and lyberall mercy
Maye graunt the gyfte, & eke thy proude enemy,
Confounded and rebuked by thy batayle,
Shall the no more happely for very fhame affayle.

But when thou mayft ones y° triumphe obtayne
Prepare thy felfe and trymme the in thy gere
As thou fholdeft incontinent fight agayn,
For yf thou be redy the devyll wyll the fere :
Wherfore in ony wyfe fo ever thou the bere

That thou remembre and have ever in memory
In victory batayle in batayle victory.

THE .IX. RULE.

If thou thynke thy felfe well fenced and fure
Agaynft every fotell fuggeftion of vyce,
Confydre frayle glaffe may no dyftres endure,
And grete adventurers ofte curs the dyce :
Jeopard not to farre therfore and ye be wyfe,
But evermore efchewe the occafyons of fynne,
For he that loveth parell fhall perefsh therin.

THE .X. RULE.

In all temptacyon withftonde the begynnynge :
The curfed infantes of wretched Babilon "
To fuffre them wax is a jeoperdous thynge :
Bete out theyr braynes therfore at the Stone :
Perylous is the canker that catcheth the bone :
To late cometh the medicine yf thou let the fore
By longe contynuaunce encreafe more & more.

THE .XI. RULE.

Though in the tyme of the batayle and warre
The conflecte feme bytter fharpe and fowre,
Yet confydre hit is more pleafure farre
Over the devyll to be a conqueroure
Then is in the ufe of thy beeftly pleafoure :
Of vertue more joye the confcience hath within
Then outwarde the body of all his fylthy fynne.

In this poynt many men erre for necligence,
For they compare not the joye of the vyctory
To the fenfuall pleafure of theyr concupifcence,

But lyke rude beeftes unadvifedly
Lakkynge difcrecyon they compare & applye
Of theyr fowle fynne the voluptuoufe delyght
To the laberous travayle of the conflyct & fyght.

And yet alas he that ofte hath knowen
What gryefe it is by longe experyence
Of his cruell enemye to be over throwen,
Sholde ones at the left wyfe do his diligence
To prove and affaye with manly defence
What pleafure there is, what honour peace & reft
In glorioufe victorye tryumphe and conqueft.

THE .XII. RULE.

Though thou be tempted difpayre the nothynge :
Remembre the gloryous apoftle Saynt Paule
Whan he had feen God in his perfyte beynge,
Left fuche revelacyon fholde his herte extolle,
His flefshe was fuffred rebell agaynft the foule :
This dyd almyghty God of his goodnes provide
To preferve his fervaunt fro ye daunger of pryde.

And here take hede that he whom God dyd love,
And for his mooft efpeciall veffell chofe,
Ravyfshed into the thyrde heven above,
Yet ftode in peryll left pryde myght hym depofe :
Well ought we then our hertes fence & clofe
Agaynft vaynglorye the mother of repryefe,
The very crop and rote of all myfchefe.

Agaynft this pompe & wretched worldes glofe
Confydre how Crift the Lorde, fovereyne powere,
Humbled him felfe for us unto the croffe :

And peradventure deth with in one houre
Shal us bereve welth ryches and honowre :
And bryng us down ful low both fmal & grete
To vyle caryon and wretched wormes mete.

Here folowe the .XII. wepens of fpirytual batayle
which every man fhuld have at hand when y⁰ plefure of
a fynful temptacyon commeth to his mynde.

The plefure lytle & fhort. Eternal joy eternal payne.
The folowers gryef & Ye nature & dygnyte of
hevynes. man.
The loffe of a bettyr thyng. Y⁰ peace of a good mynde.
This lyfe a dreame and a The grete benfytes of God.
fhadowe. The peynful cros of Cryft.
The deth at our hand & The wytnes of martyrs
unware. and example of fayntes.
Y⁰ fere of impenitent de-
partyng.

THE .XII. WEPENS HAVE WE[45] MORE AT LENGTH DECLARED AS HIT FOLOWYTH.

THE PLEASURE LYTLE AND SHORT.

Confydre well the pleafure that thou haft,
Stande hit in towchyng or in wanton fyght,
In vayne fmell or in thy lycoroufe taft,
Or fynally in what fo ever delyght
Occupyed is thy wretched appetyght :
Thou fhalt hit fynde when thou haft al caft
Lytle, fymple, fhort, and fodenly paft.

THE FOLOWERS GRYEFE & HEVYNES.

Ony good wark yf thou with labour do,
The labour goth, the goodnes doth remayne :
If thou do evyl with pleafure joyned therto,

The pleafure which thyne evyll wark doth contayne
Glydeth his wey, thou maft hym not reftrayne :
The evyl then in thy breft cleveth behynde
Wyth grudge of hert and hevynes of mynde.

THE LOSSE OF A BETTER THYNG.

When thou laboreft thy pleafure for to bye
Upon the pryce loke thou the well advyfe,
Thou felleft thy foule therfore evyn by & by
To thy mooft uttre difpiteoufe enemyes :
A mad merchaunt, o folifsh merchaundyfe,
To by a tryfle, o chyldyfshe rekenynge,
And pay therefore fo dere a precyoufe thyng.

THIS LYFE A DREME AND A SHADOW.

This wretched life (the truft & confidence
Of whofe contynuaunce maketh us bolde to fynne)
Thou perceiveft well by experience,
Sith that houre in which hit dyde begynne,
Hit holdeth on the courfe and wyll not lynne,[45]
But faft hit rynneth on and paffen fhall
As doth a dreme or a fhadowe on the wall.

DETH AT OUR HAND AND UNWARE.

Confydre well that ever nyght and daye,
Whyle that we befyly provyde and care
For oure difport revell myrth and play,
For plefaunt melody and deynty fare :
Deth ftelyth on ful flyly, and unware
He lieth at hand and fhall us entreprife
We not[47] how foone nor in what maner wife.

FERE OF IMPENITENT DEPARTYNGE.

If thou fholdeft God offende thynke how therfore
Thou were forthwith in very jeoperdous cafe
For happely thou fholdeft not lyve an houre more
Thy fynne to clenfe, & though thou haddeft fpace.
Yet peradventure fholdeft thou lacke the grace :
Well ought we then be a ferde to done offence
Impenitent left we departen hens.

ETERNALL REWARDE ETERNALL PAYNE.

Thou feeft this worlde is but a thorowfare,
Se thou behave the wifely with thy hooft :
Hens muft thou nedes departe naked & bare,
And after thy deferte loke to what cooft
Thou arte convayed at fuche tyme as thy gooft
From this wretched carkas fhall dyffever :
Be hit joye or payne, endure hit thou fhall for ever.

THE NATURE AND DYGNITE OF MAN.

Remembre how God hath made the refonable
Lyke unto his image and fygure,
And for the fuffred paynes intollerable
That he for aungell never wolde endure.
Regarde o man thyne excellent nature :
Thou that with aungell arte made to bene egall,
For very fhame be not the devylles thrall.

THE PEACE OF A GOOD MYNDE.

Why loveft thou fo this brotle worldes joye :
Take all the myrth, take all the fantafies,
Take every game, take every wanton toye,

Take every ſport that man can the devyſe :
And amonge them all on warantyſe
Thou ſhalt no pleaſure comparable ſynde
To th'ynwarde gladnes of a vertuous mynde.

THE GRETE BENEFYCES OF GOD.

By ſyde that God the bought & fourmed both
Many a benefyte haſt thou receyved of his :
Though thou have moved hym often to be wroth
Yet he the kepte hath and brought us up to this,
And dayly calleth upon the to his blys :
How mayſt thou then to hym unlovynge be
That ever hath ben ſo lovynge unto the.

THE PAYNFULL CROSSE OF CHRYST.

Whan thou in flame of the temptacyon fryeſt
Thynke on the very lamentable payne,
Thynke on the pyteouſe croſſe of wofull Chryſt,
Thynke on his blode bet out at every vayne,
Thynke on his precyous herte kerved in twayne :
Thynke how for thy redempcyon all was wrought :
Let hym not leſe that he ſo dere hath bought.

THE WYTNES OF MARTYRES & EXAMPLE OF SAYNTES.

Synne to withſtonde ſaye not thou lakkeſt myght :
Suche allegacyons folye hit is to uſe :
The wytnes of ſayntes, & martyrs conſtant fyght
Shall the of ſlouthfull cowardyſe accuſe :
God will the helpe yf thou do not refuſe :
Yf other have ſtande or this thou mayſt eft ſoone :
Nothynge impoſſible is that hath bene doone.

THE .XII. PROPERTEES OR CONDICYONS
OF A LOVER.

To love one alone and contempne all other for y' one.

To thynke hym unhappy that is not with his love.

To adourne hym felfe for the pleafure of his love.

To fuffre all thyng, thoughe hit were deth, to be with his
love.

To defyre alfo to fuffre fhame harme for his love, and to
thynke that hurte fwete.

To be with his love ever as he may, yf not in dede yet in
thought.

To love all thynge y' perteyneth unto his love.

To coveite the prayfe of his love, and not to fuffre ony
dyfprayfe.

To beleve of his love all thynges excellent, & to defyre
that all folke fholde thynke the fame.

To wepe often with his love: in prefence for joye, in
abfence for forowe.

To languyfshe ever and ever to burne in the defyre of his
love.

To ferve his love, nothyng thynkynge of ony rewarde or
profyte.

THE . XII . PROPERTEES WE HAVE AT
LENGTH MORE OPENLY EXPRESSED IN
BALADE AS HIT FOLOWETH.[48]

The fyrft poynt is to love but one alone,
And for that one all other to forfake:
For who fo loveth many loveth none:
The flode that is in many chanelles take
In eche of them fhall feble ftremes make:

The love that is devyded amonge many
Unneth fuffyfeth that ony parte have ony.

So thou that haft thy love fet unto God
In thy remembraunce this enprynt & grave :
As he in foverayne dignyte is odde,
So wyll he in love no partynge felowes have :
Love hym therfore with all that he the gave :
For body, fowle, wytte, connynge, mynde & thought,
Parte wyll he none, but eyther all or nought.

THE SECONDE PROPERTE.

Of his love lo the fyght and company
To the lover fo glad and pleafaunt is,
That who fo hath the grace to come therby
He judgeth hym in perfyte joye and blys :
And who fo of that company doth myffe,
Lyve he in never fo profperous eftate,
He thynketh hym wretched and infortunate.

So fholde the lover of God efteme that he
Whiche all the pleafure hath, myrth and difporte
That in this worlde is poffible to be,
Yet tyll the tyme that he maye ones reforte
Unto that blyffed joyfull hevenly porte
Where he of God may have the glorious fyght,
Is voyde of parfyte joye and delyght.

THE THYRDE PROPERTE.

The thyrde poynt of a parfyte lover is
To make hym frefshe, to fe that all thynge bene
Apoynted well and nothynge fet a mys,

But all well fafshoned, propre, goodly & clene:
That in his parfone there be nothynge fene
In fpeche, apparayll, gefture, loke or pace
That may offende or mynyfshe ony grace.

So thou that wylte with God gete in to favoure
Garnyfshe thy felfe up in as goodly wyfe,
As comely be, as honeft in behavoure
As hit is poffyble for the to devyfe:
I meane not hereby that thou fholdeft aryfe,
And in the glaffe upon thy body prowle,[49]
But with fayre vertue to adourne thy foule.

THE FOURTH PROPERTE.

If love be ftronge, hote, myghty, and fervent,
There may no trouble, greyfe or forow fall,
But that the lover wolde be well content
All to endure and thynke hit eke to fmall,
Thoughe hit were deth: fo he myght therwithall
The joyfull prefence of that perfone get
On whom he hath his herte and love i set.

Thus fholde of God the lover be content
Ony dyftres or forow to endure,
Rather then to be from God abfent,
And glad to dye, fo that he maye be fure
By his departynge hens for to procure
After this valey darke the hevenly lyght,
And of his love the gloryoufe fight.

THE FYFT PROPERTE.

Not onely a lover content is in his herte,
But coveyteth eke and longeth to fuftayne

Some laboure, incommodite or fmarte,
Loffe, adverfyte, trouble, greyfe or payne :
And of his forowe joyfull is and fayne,
And happy thynketh hymfelfe that he may take
Some myfadventure for his lovers fake.

Thus fholdeft thou that loveft God alfo
In thyne herte wyfshe, coveyte and be glad
For hym to fuffre trouble, payne and woo :
For whom yf thou be never fo woo beftade,
Yet thou ne fhalt fufteyne (be not adrad)
Halfe the dolour, gryefe and adverfyte
The he all redy fuffred hath for the.

THE . VI . PROPERTE.

The parfyte lover longeth for to be
In prefence of his love both nyght & daye :
And yf hit happely fo be fall that he
May not as he wolde : he wyl yet as he may
Ever be with his love, that is to faye,
Where his hevy body nyl be brought [50]
He wyll be converfaunt in mynd and thought.

Lo in lyke maner the lover of God fholde
At the left in fuche wyfe as he may,
If he may not in fuche wyfe as he wolde,
Be prefent with God and converfaunt alway :
For certes who fo lyft he may purvey,
Though al yᵉ worlde wolde hym therfro beryven,
To bere his body in erth, his mynde in heven.

THE . VII . PROPERTE.

There is no page or fervaunt moft or left
That doth upon his love attende & wayte,

There is no lytle worme, no fymple beft,
Ne none fo fmall a tryfle or conceyte,
Lafe, gyrdell, poynt, or propre glove ftrayte :
But that yf to his love hit have ben nere,
The lover hath hit precyous, leyfe, & dere.

So every relyque, image or pycture,
That doth pertayne to Goddes magnyfycence,
The lover of God fholde wyth all befy cure
Have hit in love, honoure and reverence :
And fpecyally gyve them preemynence
Which dayly done his bleffed body nyrche,[51]
The quyk relyques, the mynyftres of his chyrch.

THE . VIII. PROPERTE.

A very lover above all erthly thyng
Coveyteth and longeth evermore to here
T'honoure, lawde, commendacyon and prayfyng,
And every thyng that may the fame clere
Of his love : he may in no manere
Endure to here that therefro myghten vary,
Or ony thyng fowne in to the contrary.

The lover of God fholde coveyte in lyke wyfe
To here his honoure, worfhyp, laude and prayfe,
Whofe fovereygne goodnes none herte may compryfe,
Whom hell, erth, and all the heven obayfe :
Whofe parfyte lover ought by no maner wayes
To fuffre the curfed wordes of blafphemy,
Or ony thynge fpoken of God unreverently.

THE . IX . PROPERTE.

A very lover beleveth in his mynde,
On whom fo ever he hath his herte i bent,

That in that perſone men may nothynge fynde
But honorable, worthy and excellent,
And eke ſurmountynge farre in his entent
All other that he hath knowen by ſyght or name :
And wolde that every man ſholde thynke the ſame.

Of God lyke wyſe ſo wonderfull and hye
All thynge eſteme & judge his lover ought,
So reverence, worſhyp, honour & magnyfye,
That all the creatures in this worlde i wrought
In comparyſon ſholde hee ſet at nought :
And glad be yf he myght the meane devyſe
That all the worlde wolde thynken in lyke wyſe.

THE . X . PROPERTE.

The lover is of colour deed and pale :
There wyll no ſlepe in to his eyen ſtalk :
He favoreth neyther mete, wyne, nor ale :
He myndeth not what men about hym talke :
But ete he, drynke he, syt, lye downe or walke,
He burneth ever as hit were with a fyre
In the ſervent hete of his deſyre.

Here ſholde the lover of God enſample take
To have hym contynually in remembraunce,
With hym in prayer and medytacyon wake,
Whyle other playe, revell, ſynge, and daunce :
None erthly joy, diſport or vayne pleſaunce
Solde hym delyte, or ony thynge remove
His ardent mynde from God his hevynly love.

THE . XI . PROPERTE.

Dyverſly paſſyoned is the lovers herte :
Now pleſaunt hope, now drede and grevous ſere,
Now parfyte blyſſe, now bytter ſorowe ſmarte :
And whether his love be with hym or elles where,
Oſt from his eyen there ſalleth many a tere :
For very joy when they togyther be :
Whan they be ſondred for adverſyte.

Lyke affeccyons ſeleth eke the breſt
Of Goddes lover in prayer and meditacyon :
Whan that his love lyketh in hym reſt
With inwarde gladnes of pleaſaunt contemplacyon,
Out breke the teres ſor joye and delectacyon :
And whan his love lyſt eſte to parte hym fro,
Out breke the teres agayne for payne & woo.

THE .XII. PROPERTE.

A very lover wyll his love obaye :
His joye it is and all his appetyght
To payne hym ſelfe in all that ever he maye,
That parſone in whom he ſet hathe his delyght
Dylygent to ſerve bothe day and nyght
For very love without ony regarde
To ony profyte, gwerdon or rewarde.

So thou lyke wyſe that haſt thyne herte i ſet
Upwarde to God : ſo well thy ſelfe endevere,
So ſtudyouſly that nothynge may the let
Nor fro his ſervyce ony wyſe diſſevere :
Frely loke eke thou ſerve that therto never

Truſt of rewarde or profyte do the bynde,
But onely faythfull herte & lovynge mynde.

Wageles to ſerve .iii. thynges may us move :
Fyrſt yf the ſervyce ſelfe be defyrable :
Seconde yf they whom that we ſerve & love
Be very good and very amyable :
Thyrdely of reaſon be we ſervyſable
Without the gapynge after ony more
To ſuche as have done moche for us before.

Serve God for love then, not for hope of mede.
What ſervyce maye ſo defyrable be
As where all turneth to thyne owne ſpede.
Who is ſo good, ſo lovely eke as he,
Who hath all redy done ſo moche for the,
As he that fyrſt the made, and on the rode
Eft the redemed with his precyous blode.

A PRAYER OF PICUS MIRANDULA UNTO GOD.

O holy God of dredefull mageſtee
Verely one in .iii . and thre in one :
Whom aungelles ſerve, whoſe werk all creatures be,
Which heven and erth directeſt all alone :
We The beſeche good Lorde with wofull mone,
Spare us wretches & waſshe away our gylt
That we be not by thy juſt angre ſpylt.

In ſtraye balance of rygorous judgement
If Thou ſholdeſt our ſynne pondre and wey :
Who able were to bere thy punyſshment.

The hole engyne of all this worlde I faye,
The engyne that enduren fhall for aye,
With fuche examynacyon myght not ftande
Space of a moment in thyne angry hande.

Who is not born in fynne originall.
Who doth not actuall fynne in fondry wyfe.
But thou good Lorde arte he that fpareft all
With pyteoufe mercy temperynge juftyce :
For as Thou doeft rewardes us devyce
Above our meryte, fo doeft thou difpence
Thy punyfshement farre undre our offence.

More is thy mercy farre then all our fynne :
To gyve them alfo that unworthy be
More godly is, and more mercy therin.
Howbehit worthy inough are they perdee :
Be they never fo unworthy : whom that he
Lyft to accept : where fo ever he taketh
Whom he unworthy fyndeth worthy maketh.

Wherfore good Lorde that aye mercyfull arte,
Unto thy grace and foverayne dygnyte
We fely wretches crye with humble herte :
Oure fynnes forget and our malygnite :
With pyteous eyes of thy benygnyte
Frendly loke on us ones thyne owne,
Servauntes or fynners whether hit lyketh The.

Synners, yf Thou our cryme beholde, certayne :
Our cryme the warke of our uncorteyfe mynde :
But yf thy gyftes Thou beholde agayne,
Thy gyftes noble wonderfull and kynde :

Thou ſhalte us then the ſame perſones fynde
Which are to The, and have be longe ſpace
Servauntes by nature, chyldren by thy grace.

But this thy goodnes wryngeth us alas:
For we whom grace had made thy chyldren dere
Are made thy gylty folke by our treſpace:
Synne hath us gylty made this many a yere.
But let thy grace, thy grace that hath no pere,
Of our offence ſurmounten all the peace,[52]
That in our ſynne thyne honour may encreace.

For though thy wiſdom, though thy ſoverayn powre
May other wyſe appere ſuffycyently:
As thynges whiche thy creatures every houre
All with one voice declare and teſtyfye:
Thy goodnes yet, thy ſynguler mercy,
Thy pyteous herte, thy gracyous indulgence
Nothynge ſo clerely ſheweth as our offence.

What but our ſynne hath ſhewed that mighty love:
Whiche able was thy dredful mageſtee
To drawe downe in to erth fro heven above
And crucyfye God: that we poor wretches we
Sholde from our fylthy ſynne iclenſed be
With blode and water of thyne owne ſyde,
That ſtremed from thy blyſſed woundes wyde.

Thy love and pyte thus o hevenly Kynge
Our evyll maketh mater of thy goodnes.
O love, o pyte, our welth ay provydynge,
O goodnes ſervyng thy ſervauntes in diſtres.
O love, o pyte, well nygh now thankles.

O goodnes, myghty, gracyous and wyſe,
And yet almoſt now vanquyſshed with our vyce.

Graunt I The praye ſuche hete into myne herte
That to this love of thyne may be egall.
Graunt me fro Sathanas ſervyce to aſtert,
With whom me rueth ſo longe to be thrall.
Graunt me good Lorde and Creatour of all
The flame to quenche of all ſynfull deſyre,
And in thy love ſet all myne herte a fyre.

That whan the journay of this deedly lyfe
My ſely gooſt hath fynyſshed, and thenſe
Departen muſt without his fleſshly wyſe,
Alone in to his Lordes hygh preſence :
He may The fynde : o Well of Indulgence :
In thy lordeſhyp not as a lorde : but rather
As a very tendre lovynge father.
      Amen.

Enprynted at London in the Fleteſtrete
at the ſygne of the Sonne, by me
Wynkyn de Worde.

NOTES.

NOTES.

COLLATION OF MORE'S TEXT with the original showed that in a few instances he had inaccurately or inadequately rendered it. In such cases, or where for any other reason it seemed desirable, the words of the original are given in the notes, the letters G. F. P. or P. subjoined in brackets indicating that the reference is to the Latin life by Giovanni Francesco Pico or to Pico's works. A few misprints have been silently corrected.

1. This lady may be either Jocosa or Joyce, daughter of Richard Culpeper of Hollingborne, Kent, and wife of Ralph Leigh, undersheriff of London, or her daughter, Jocosa or Joyce Leigh, sister of Sir John Leigh who succeeded to the manor of Stockwell, Surrey, on the death of his uncle, Sir John Leigh, 27 Aug., 1523. Tanswell, "History and Antiquities of Lambeth," pp. 41-2. Manning and Bray, "History of Surrey," iii. 497-8.

2. Pico was the third son and youngest child of Giovanni Francesco Pico, Count of Mirandola and Concordia in the Modenese. He had two brothers, Galeotto, and Antonio Maria, and three sisters, Catterina, Lucrezia and

M

Giulia.   Galeotto had to wife Bianca, daughter of Niccolò
d'Este, lord of Ferrara; Antonio Maria married twice, viz.,
(1) Costanza, daughter of Sante Bentivoglio, lord of
Bologna, (2) a Neapolitan lady.   Pico's eldest sister,
Catterina, married (1) Leonello Pio, lord of Carpi, by
whom she had Alberto, mentioned in connection with
Pico's death; (2) Rodolfo, lord of Gonzaga.   Carpi and
Gonzaga are little towns in the Modenese.   Lucrezia
also married twice, viz. (1) Pino Ordelaffo, lord of
Forli; (2) Gherardo Appiani di Piombino, Count of
Montagnana.   The third sister, Giulia, took the veil.

Pico's pedigree has been carried back as far as Manfredo
of Reggio, a contemporary of Charlemagne; but the descent from the nephew of Constantine is mythical.

"Memorie Storiche della Mirandola," Litta, "Celebr.
Fam. Ital."   Pico, *Opera* (ed. 1601), *Life* by G. F. Pico;
and "Adversus Astrologos," ii. cap. ix.

3. The Boiardi.   Giulia was the daughter of Feltrino
Boiardo, first Count of Scandiano, and aunt of the poet,
Matteo Maria Boiardo, author of the "Orlando Innamo-
rato." Litta, "Celebr. Fam. Ital." Venturi, "Storia di
Scandiano," p. 83.

4. Paulinus was secretary to S. Ambrose, and wrote
his life; from which the story in the text is taken.

5. "Flavo et inaffectato capillitio" (G. F. P.).   Apparently Pico was somewhat careless about the arrangement
of his hair.

6. Apollonius of Tyana, fl. 70 A.D., travelled throughout the ancient world expounding Neo-Pythagoreanism,
and working wonders, esteemed miraculous.

7. For an account of these spurious compositions,
written at various dates between the first century before
and the third century after Christ, but which were uni-

versally regarded as genuine in Pico's day, see Zeller, "Philosophie der Griechen."

8. Aquinas.

9. With whom Pico was connected by affinity. See note 2.

10. For this vaunt of Epicurus see Diogenes Laertius, "Vitæ Philosph." x. 13 sc. τοῦτον Ἀπολλόδωρος ἐν χρονικοῖς Λυσιφάνους ἀκοῦσαί φησι καὶ Πραξιφάνους· αὐτὸς δὲ οὔ φησιν ἀλλ' ἑαυτοῦ, ἐν τῇ πρὸς Εὐρύδικον ἐπιστολῇ.

11. Pico's conduct in this matter was not altogether so generous as it appears in the text. Soon after his father's death his brothers had fallen out about the partition of the family estates, and matters went so far that in 1473 Galeotto surprised Antonio Maria and incarcerated him in the citadel of Mirandola, while he made himself master of the entire inheritance, apparently ignoring Pico's title altogether. Antonio Maria remained a close prisoner in Mirandola for about two years, at the close of which he was released in deference to the intercessions, or perhaps menaces, of his friends, fled to Rome, and appealed to the Pope. He returned in 1483 with a small army furnished by the Duke of Calabria, possessed himself of Concordia, and negotiated a treaty of partition with his brother. The treaty was, however, by no means strictly observed. Pico had taken no part in the quarrel, and was probably the more ready to cede his rights to his nephew that any attempt to vindicate them for himself would certainly have excited the determined hostility of his brothers. The conveyance was executed on 22 April 1491. "Memorie Storiche della Mirandola," i. 108 ; ii. 43. Calori Cesis, "Giovanni Pico."

12. Girolamo Benivieni, author of the "Canzone dell'

Amore Celeste e Divino" on which Pico wrote the commentary referred to in the Introduction p. 24. For an account of him see Mazzucchelli, "Scrittori Italiani."

13. St. Jerome, author of the Vulgate version of the Bible. The passage referred to is as follows :—" Scimus plerosque dedisse eleemosynam, sed de proprio corpore nihil dedisse ; porrexisse egentibus manum, sed carnis voluptate superatos dealbasse ea quae foris erant, et intus plenos fuisse ossibus mortuorum." "Epistola ad Eustochium Virginem," *Opera* (fol.) i. 65. g.

14. "Potissimum" (G. F. P.), especially. So in "Romaunt of the Rose," l. 1,358-9, the pomegranate is described as a fruyt fulle well to lyke, "*Namely*, to folk whanne they ben sike."

15. A reminiscence of the "De Sapientis Constantia."

16. "Passim" (G. F. P.), on all hands. In fourteenth and fifteenth century literature "by and by" frequently means severally, or one by one, as in "Romaunt of the Rose," l. 4,582, "These were his wordis by and by." The "Promptorum Parvulorum" (Camden Soc.) translates it "sigillatim." Thence the transition to the sense of the text is not difficult.

17. See Introduction, p. xxiii.

18. "Quam primum" (G. F. P.), as soon as possible.

19. See note 6.

20. A reminiscence of Epode II.

21. After leaving Bologna, Pico spent two years at Padua, the stronghold of scholasticism in Italy. He also studied for a time at Ferrara, under Battista Guarino, the humanist, whom in one of his letters he addresses as *præceptor meus*. In 1482 he returned to Mirandola, in the vicinity of which he built himself a little villa, which

he describes as " pleasant enough, considering the nature of the place and district," and on which he wrote a poem now lost. Here he entertained Aldo Manuzio, who about the same time, doubtless by Pico's recommendation, was appointed tutor to his nephew, Alberto Pio, and a Greek scholar, Emanuel Adramyttenus, a refugee from Crete, where the Moslem was triumphant. He now began to correspond with Politian, and on a visit to Reggio made the acquaintance of Savonarola, who had come thither to attend a chapter of Dominicans. In 1483 he went to Pavia, taking with him Emanuel Adramyttenus, who acted as his Greek master. There Emanuel died, and Pico then joined Aldo Manuzio at Carpi. About this time he began the study of the oriental languages, his master being one Jocana, otherwise unknown. In 1484, if not earlier, he went to Florence, and made himself known to Marsilio Ficino, who had then just completed his translation of Plato. Pico urged him to crown his labours by performing the same office for Plotinus. Ficino, who was so little above the common superstitions of his time that he believed firmly in astrology, saw in Pico's unexpected appearance at this critical juncture an event not to be explained by natural causes, and taking his suggestion as a divine monition, forthwith set about the work : nor, when it was completed, did he omit to recount, in dedicating it to Lorenzo, the incident which led to its initiation. Pico appears to have remained at Florence until the latter part of 1485, when we lose sight of him for a time. We obtain, however, a transient glimpse of him in a somewhat novel light from a letter from his sister-in-law, Costanza, to Fra Girolamo, of Piacenza, dated 16 May, 1486, and printed in " Memorie Storiche della Mirandola," ii. 167. From this it appears that he had then recently left Arezzo with a Florentine married lady, who, Costanza is careful to state, "accompanied him voluntarily," but had been attacked by some boors, who cut to pieces his attendants, wounded him in two places, and carried him back to Arezzo. Whether the outrage is imputable to the jealousy of the lady's husband, Costanza cannot say. How the affair ended does not appear, but in the following October we find Pico at Perugia, and in November at Fratta in the Ferrarese. Then followed the visit to Rome, the affair of the Theses, and the journey to France, where he was presented to Charles VIII. After his recall to Italy he resided either at Fiesole or Florence until the summer of 1491, when he accompanied Politian to Venice. They returned to Florence in time to be present at the deathbed of Lorenzo (8 Ap. 1492). The rest of his life Pico spent partly at Ferrara and partly at Florence.

The foregoing brief record of Pico's wanderings reposes mainly upon the evidence afforded by his letters and those of Aldo Manuzio, Politian, and Ficino. Many of these, however, are undated, and all are singularly poor in personal detail. See also Calori Cesis, "Giovanni Pico della Mirandola," 2nd ed., 1872 ; Parr Greswell, "Memoirs of Angelus Politianus," &c. ; and Villari's "Savonarola," Eng. tr. 1889, ii. 74.

22. "Insidiosissima correptus est febre" (G. F. P.), "Axes" is of course merely *access*.

23. See Note 2.

24. "Cæli reginam ad se nocte adventasse miro fragrantem odore, membraque omnia febre illa *contusa contractaque* refovisse" (G. F. P.).   "Brosed" = bruised ("contusa").   "Frushed" appears to be derived from the

French *froisser*, which may mean either to bruise or to rumple ; whence also probably "froyse" used locally for a pancake. See "Promptorium Parvulorum" (Camden Soc.) *Froyse.*

25. See note 2.

26. Charles VIII., to whom Pico had recently been presented. See note 21.

27. Girolamo Savonarola. For what little is known of his relations with Pico see note 21, and his life by Villari, Eng. tr. (1889).

28. "Verum divinis beneficiis male gratus, vel ab sensibus vocatus, detractabat labores (delicatæ quippe temperaturæ fuerat) ; vel arbitratus eius opera religionem indigere, differebat ad tempus : hoc tamen non ut verum sed ut a me conjectatum et præsumptum dixerim" (G. F. P.). But unmindful of God's favours to him, or led away by the senses, he shrank from the labours (he was of a delicate constitution) ; or thinking that religion had need of his services he yet deferred them for a time : not, however, that I state this as truth, but only as what I conjecture or presume to be so.

29. "A diaboli laqueis" (P.), from the snares of the devil. So in Holinshed, "History of Scotland," Ethodius, 194 H. B., we read of "nets and grens" for snaring hares.

30. "Suggeret tibi cum Spiritus qui interpellat pro nobis, tum ipsa necessitas singulis horis quod petas a Deo tuo : suggeret et sacra lectio, quam ut omissis jam fabulis nugisque poetarum semper habeas in manibus etiam atque etiam rogo" (P.). It shall be taught thee both by the Spirit which intercedes for us and by thine own needs every hour what thou shouldest ask of thy God ; and also by the reading of the holy scriptures, which, laying now

aside the frivolous fables of the poets, I earnestly entreat thee to have ever in thy hands.

31. The letter is dated from Ferrara, 15 May, 1492, *i.e.* shortly after the death of Lorenzo.

32. A fragment of the lost Neoptolemus of Ennius :—

"Philosophari est mihi necesse, at paucis, nam omnino haut placet ;
Degustandum ex ea, non in eam ingurgitandum censeo."

Ribbeck, "Frag. Lat. Reliq." i. 53 ; cf. Cic. "Tusc. Dispt." ii. 1.

33. Epist I. i. *ad fin :*—

"Ad summam : sapiens uno minor est Jove, dives,
Liber, honoratus, pulcher, rex denique regum ;
Præcipue sanus, nisi cum pituita molesta est."

34. " Uti mannus" (P.), like a draught-horse. Doubtless in More's edition the word was spelt mānus ; hence the curious mistranslation.

35. "*Perusiæ* xv. Octo Mcccclxxx*vi*. anno gratiæ" (P.). It is not easy to account for the double error into which More has here fallen.

36. " Mentientes *propter* eum " (P.), lying (*i.e.* to our disadvantage) because of him.

37. Ps. xxv. 1-5 in the authorized and revised versions. The Vulgate, where it appears as Ps. xxiv., has a slightly different rendering :—"Ad Te Domine levavi animam meam : Deus meus in Te confido, non erubescam : Neque irrideant me inimici mei : etenim universi, qui sustineant Te, non confundentur. Dirige me in veritate tua, et doce me, quia Tu es Deus Salvator meus, et Te sustinui tota die."

38. Ps. xvi. in the authorized and revised versions, xv. in the Vulgate, which is as follows :—"Conserva me Domine, quoniam speravi in Te. Dixi Domino : Deus

meus es Tu, quoniam bonorum meorum non eges. Sanctis qui sunt in terra ejus mirificavit omnes voluntates meas in eis. Multiplicatæ sunt infirmitates eorum : postea acceleraverunt. Non congregabo conventicula eorum de sanguinibus : nec memor ero nominum eorum per labia mea. Dominus pars hereditatis meæ, et calicis mei. Tu es qui restitues hereditatem meam mihi. Funes ceciderunt mihi in præclaris : etenim hereditas mea præclara est mihi. Benedicam Dominum, qui tribuit mihi intellectum : insuper et usque ad noctem increpuerunt me renes mei. Providebam Dominum in conspectu meo semper : quoniam a dextris est mihi ne commovear. Propter hoc lætatum est cor meum, et exultavit lingua mea : insuper et caro mea requiescet in spe. Quoniam non derelinques animam meam in inferno : nec dabis sanctum tuum videre corruptionem. Notas mihi fecisti vias vitæ, adimplebis me lætitia cum vultu tuo : delectationes in dextera tua usque in finem."

39. "By-and-by" is here evidently *forthwith*, and "medyatly" *immediately*.

40. These rules, of which More's verses are rather a paraphrase than a translation, were written by Pico in prose, and were translated into prose by Sir Thomas Elyot, author of the "Boke of the Governour," as follows :

"THE RULES OF A CHRISTIAN LYFE MADE BY JOHAN PICUS THE ELDER ERLE OF MIRANDULA.

"Firſt if to man or woman the way of vertue dothe feme harde or paynefull, bycaufe we mufte nedes fyghte agaynfte the flefhe, the divell, and the worlde, lette hym

or her calle to remembraunce, that what fo ever lyfe they
wyll chofe accordynge to the worlde, many adverfities,
incommodities, moche hevynes and labour are to be
fuffred.

"Moreover lette them have in remembraunce, that in
welth and worldly poffeffions is moche and longe conten-
tion, laborioufe alfo, and ther with unfrutefulle, wherin
travayle is the conclufyon or ende of labour, and fynally
payne everlaftynge, if thofe thynges be not well ordered
and charitably difpofed.

"Remembre alfo, that it is very folifhnes to thinke to
come unto heven by any other meane than by the fayde
batayle, confidering that our hed and mayfter Chrifte did
not afcende unto heven but by his paffion : And the fer-
vaunte oughte not to be in better aftate or condicion than
his mayfter or foverayne.

"Furthermore confyder, that this bataile ought not to
be grudged at, but to be defired and wifhed for, all though
thereof no price or rewarde mought enfue or happen, but
onely that therby we mought be conformed or joyned to
Chrifte our God and mayfter. Wherefore as often as in
refiftinge any temptacion thou dooeft withftande any of
the fences or wittes, thinke unto what part of Chriftes
paffion thou mayfte applye thy felfe or make thy felfe
lyke : As refiftinge glotony, whiles thou doeft punyfhe
thy taft or appetite : remembre that Chrifte receyved in
his drynke ayfelle myxte with the gall of a beafte, a
drinke mofte unfavery and loathfome. Whan thou with-
drawefte thy hande from unlefull takinge or kepinge of
any thinge, whiche liketh thyne appetite : remembre
Chriftes handis as they were faft nayled unto the tree of
the croffe. And refifting of pryde, thinke on him, who
being very God almighty, for thy fake received the forme

of a ſubjecte, and humbled hym ſelfe unto the mooſte vile
and reproachefull deathe of the croſſe.

"And whan thou art tempted with wrathe : remembre
that He whiche was God, and of all men the moſt juſte
or rightwyſe, whan He behelde hym ſelfe mocked, ſpit
on, ſcourged, and puniſhed with alle diſpites and rebukes,
and ſette on the croſſe amonge errant theves, as if He
Hym Selfe were a falſe harlot, He notwithſtanding ſhewed
never token of indignacion or that He were greved, but
ſuffering al thinges with wonderful pacience, aunſwered
al men moſt gentilly. In this wiſe if thou peruſe al
thinges one after an other, thou mayſt finde, that there is
no paſſion or trouble, that ſhall not make the in ſome
parte conformable or like unto Chriſte.

"Alſo putte not thy truſte in mannes helpe, but in the
onelye vertue of Chriſte Jeſu, whiche ſayde : Truſte well,
for I have vaynquiſhid the worlde. And in an other
place He ſayde : The prince of this worlde is caſte oute
thereof. Wherfore let us truſte by his onelye vertue, to
vaynquiſhe the worlde, and to ſubdue the divell. And
therfore oughte we to aſke his helpe by the prayers of us
and of his ſainctes.

" Remembre alſo, that as ſoone as thou haſt vanquiſhed
one temtation, alway an other is to be lóked for : The
divell goeth alwaye aboute and ſeketh for hym whome he
wolde devoure. Wherfore we ought to ſerve dyly-
gently and be ever in feare, and to ſay with the prophete :
I will ſtande alwaye at my defence.

" Take heed more over, that not onelye thou be not
vaynquiſhed of the dyvel, that temptith the, but alſo that
thou vanquiſhe and overcome him.   And that is not onlye
whan thou doeſte no ſyn, but alſo whan of that thinge
wherin he tempted the, thou takeſt occaſion for to do good.

As if he offrith to the fome good acte to be done to the
intent that therby thou mayfte fall into vayneglory :
furth with thou thinkinge it not to be thy deede or warke,
but the benefitte or rewarde of God, humble thou thy
felfe, and judge the to be unkynde unto God in respecte
of his manyfolde benefytes.

"As often as thou doeft fyghte, fyght as in hope to vanquifhe, & to have atte the lafte perpetualle peace. For
that paradventure God of his abundante grace fhal gyve
unto the, and the divell beynge confufid of thy victory,
fhall retorne no more agayne. But yet whan thou hafte vayn-
quifhid, beare thy felfe fo as if thou fholdeft fighte agayne
fhortly. Thus alway in battayle thou mufte thinke on
victory : and after victory thou muft prepare the to bataile
immediately.

"All though thou feleft thy felfe wil armed and redy, yet
flee notwethstandynge all occafyons to fynne. For as the
wife man faith : who loveth perylle fhall therein peryfhe.

"In all temptations refyfte the begynnynge, and beate
the children of Babilon againe the Stone, which Stone is
Chrifte, and the chyldren be yvell thoughtes and imagi-
nations. For in longe contynuinge of fynne, feldome
warketh medycyne or remedy.

"Remembre, that althoughe in the fayde conflicte of
temptation the battayle feemeth to be verye daungeroufe :
yet confyder howe moche fweter it is to vanquifhe temptation, than to folowe finne, wherto fhe inclyneth the,
wherof the ende is repentance. And herein many be foule
deceyved, whiche compare not the fwetneffe of victory to
the fwetneffe of fynne, but onely compareth battayle to pleafure. Not withftandyng a man or woman, whiche hathe a
thoufande times knowen what it is to gyve place to temptation, fhoulde ones affaye, what it is to vanquifhe temptation.

"If thou be tempted, thynke thou not therfore that God hathe forfaken the, or that he fetteth but lyttell by the, or that thou art not in the fight of God good or perfecte: but remembre, that after Sayncte Paule hadde feene God, as He was in his divinitie, and fuche fecrete mifteryes as be not lefull for any man to fpeake or reherce, he for all that fuffred temptation of the flefhe, wherwith God fuffred hym to be tempted, left he fhoulde be affaulted with pryde. Wherin a man ought to confider that Saynt Paule, which was the pure veffell of election, and rapte in to the thyrde heven, was not withftandynge in perylle to be proude of his vertues, as he faith of hym felfe. Wherfore above al temptations manne or woman oughte to arme theym moofte ftronglye agaynfte the temptation of pryde, fens pryde is the rote of all myfchyfe, agaynfte the whiche the onelye remedye is to thynke alway that God humbled hym felfe for us unto the croffe. And more over that deth hath fo humbled us whether we wyl or no, that our bodyes fhal be the meate of wormes lothefome and venymoufe."

41. "Recordare illum felle potatum et aceto" (P.). For "eysell" cf. Shakespeare, Hamlet, v. i. 1. 264, "Woo't drink up eisel?" and Sonnet, cxi. 1. 10, "Potions of eisel 'gainst my strong infection."

42. "Wood" or *wode* in the sense of *mad* is not uncommon in our older writers. So Demetrius in "A Midsummer Night's Dream," ii. 1, l. 192,

> "And here am I, and wode within this wood,
> Because I cannot find my Hermia."

43. "Preace" would seem to be a corruption of *prest*, ready, used substantivally, "put thyself in preace" mean-

ing *make thyself ready*.   See Skeat, " Etymological Dictionary of the English Language," art. *Press*.

44. Cf. Ps. cxxxvii. 8, 9: "O daughter of Babylon, who art to be destroyed; happy shall he be, that rewardeth thee as thou hast served us.   Happy shall he be, that taketh and dasheth thy little ones against the stones."

45. Here More speaks in *propria persona*, with perhaps a *double entendre* in the " We More."   There is nothing in Pico corresponding to the verses which follow.

46. For "lynne," cease, cf. Spenser, " Faery Queen," i. canto v. 35.

> "And Sisiphus an huge round stone did reele
> Against an hill, ne might from labour lin."

47. "Not" is for *ne wot*, *i.e.* know not.   So Chaucer concludes the description of the Merchant in the Prologue to the " Canterbury Tales," l. 286 :

> "But soth to sayn I n'ot how men him call." ·

48. The stanzas on the " Propertees " are original except the last two, which are a paraphrase of the following sentence :—

"Solemns autem ad hoc induci præcipue ex tribus causis.   Prima est quando servitium ipsum per se est appetibile : secunda quando ille cui servimus est in se valde bonus et amabilis : sicut solemus dicere, servimus illi propter suas virtutes. Tertia est quando ille prius quam inciperes multa tibi beneficia contulit.   Et hæc tria sunt in Deo : quia pro servitio ejus nihil naviter accipitur quod non sit nobis bonum : et quoad animam et quoad corpus : quia servire ei non est aliud quam tendere ad eum : hoc est ad summum bonum.   Similiter ipse est optimus et pulcherrimus et sapientissimus : et habet omnes conditiones quæ solent nos movere ad amandum aliquem et serviendum ei gratis : et in nos contulit summa beneficia cum nos et ex nihilo creaverit et per sanguinem Filii ab inferno redemerit." (P.) There are, moreover, three principal considerations by which we are accustomed to be impelled to this service. The first is that the service itself is desirable for its own sake. The second arises when he whom we serve is in himself very good and amiable, and we serve him, as we are in the habit of saying, on account of his virtues. The third, when before the commencement of your service he whom you serve has conferred on you many favours. And these three considerations coexist in the case of God, for nothing whatever is accepted by way of His service which is not for our good both of soul and of body: for to serve Him is nothing else but to seek after Him : *i.e.* after the chief good. Likewise He Himself is of all beings the best, and most lovely and wisest : and has in Himself all the properties which are wont to move us to love and serve any one without reward : and has conferred on us the greatest favours, since He has both created us from nothing, and redeemed us from hell by the blood of His Son."

48. Cf. "Promptorium Parvulorum" (Camd. Soc.). "Prollynge, or sekynge. Perscrutatio, investigatio, scrutinum :" and Chaucer, "Canterbury Tales," l. 16880. "Though ye prolle ay, ye shal it never find."

50. Cf. note 47.

51. "Nyrche" has been substituted by way of conjectural emendation for "*wyrche*," which is unintelligible. "Nyrche" as = nourish gives the sort of sense required by the context ; and the eccentric spelling may be merely due to the roughness with which the r was pronounced in More's time.

52. "Peace," cup: from the low Latin, *pecia*. See "Promptorium Parvulorum" (Camden Soc.) *Pece* ; and Du Cange, *Pecia*.

"Yesterday's Treasures for Today's Readers"

Titles by Benediction Classics available from Amazon.co.uk

Religio Medici, Hydriotaphia, Letter to a Friend, Thomas Browne

Pseudodoxia Epidemica: Or, Enquiries into Commonly Presumed Truths, Thomas Browne

The Maid's Tragedy, Beaumont and Fletcher

The Custom of the Country, Beaumont and Fletcher

Philaster Or Love Lies a Bleeding, Beaumont and Fletcher

A Treatise of Fishing with an Angle,   Dame Juliana Berners.

Pamphilia to Amphilanthus, Lady Mary Wroth

The Compleat Angler, Izaak Walton

The Magnetic Lady, Ben Jonson

Every Man Out of His Humour, Ben Jonson

The Masque of Blacknesse. The Masque of Beauty,. Ben Jonson

The Life of St. Thomas More, William Roper

Pendennis, William Makepeace Thackeray

Salmacis and Hermaphroditus attributed to Francis Beaumont

Friar Bacon and Friar Bungay Robert Greene

Holy Wisdom, Augustine Baker

The Jew of Malta and the Massacre at Paris, Christopher Marlowe

Tamburlaine the Great, Parts 1 & 2 AND Massacre at Paris, Christopher Marlowe

All Ovids Elegies, Lucans First Booke, Dido Queene of Carthage, Hero and Leander, Christopher Marlowe

The Titan, Theodore Dreiser

Scapegoats of the Empire: The true story of the Bushveldt Carbineers, George Witton

All Hallows' Eve, Charles Williams

My Apprenticeship: Volumes I and II, Beatrice Webb

Last and First Men / Star Maker, Olaf Stapledon

Last and First Men, Olaf Stapledon

Darkness and the Light, Olaf Stapledon

The Worst Journey in the World, Apsley Cherry-Garrard

The Schoole of Abuse, Containing a Pleasaunt Invective Against Poets, Pipers, Plaiers, Iesters and Such Like Catepillers of the Commonwelth, Stephen Gosson

Russia in the Shadows, H. G. Wells

Wild Swans at Coole, W. B. Yeats

A hundreth good pointes of husbandrie, Thomas Tusser

The Collected Works of Nathanael West: "The Day of the Locust", "The Dream Life of Balso Snell", "Miss Lonelyhearts", "A Cool Million", Nathanael West

Miss Lonelyhearts & The Day of the Locust, Nathaniel West

The Worst Journey in the World, Apsley Cherry-Garrard

Scott's Last Expedition, V1, R. F. Scott

The Dream of Gerontius, John Henry Newman

The Brother of Daphne, Dornford Yates

The Poetry of Architecture: Or the Architecture of the Nations of Europe Considered in Its Association with Natural Scenery and National Character, John Ruskin

The Downfall of Robert Earl of Huntington, Anthony Munday

Clayhanger, Arnold Bennett

South: The Story of Shackleton's Last Expedition 1914-1917, Sir Ernest Shackketon

Greene's Groatsworth of Wit: Bought With a Million of Repentance, Robert Greene

Beau Sabreur, Percival Christopher Wren

The Hekatompathia, or Passionate Centurie of Love, Thomas Watson

The Art of Rhetoric, Thomas Wilson

Stepping Heavenward, Elizabeth Prentiss

Barker's Delight, or The Art of Angling, Thomas Barker
The Napoleon of Notting Hill, G.K. Chesterton

The Douay-Rheims Bible (The Challoner Revision)

Endimion - The Man in the Moone, John Lyly

Gallathea and Midas, John Lyly,

Manners, Custom and Dress During the Middle Ages and During the Renaissance Period, Paul Lacroix

Obedience of a Christian Man, William Tyndale

St. Patrick for Ireland, James Shirley

The Wrongs of Woman; Or Maria/Memoirs of the Author of a Vindication of the Rights of Woman, Mary Wollstonecraft and William Godwin

De Adhaerendo Deo. Of Cleaving to God, Albertus Magnus

Obedience of a Christian Man, William Tyndale

A Trick to Catch the Old One, Thomas Middleton

A Yorkshire Tragedy, Thomas Middleton (attrib.)

The Princely Pleasures at Kenelworth Castle, George Gascoigne

The Fair Maid of the West. Part I and Part II. Thomas Heywood

Proserpina, Volume I and Volume II. Studies of Wayside Flowers, John Ruskin

The Endeavour Journal of Sir Joseph Banks. Sir Joseph Banks

Christ Legends: And Other Stories, Selma Lagerlof; (trans. Velma Swanston Howard)

Chamber Music, James Joyce

Blurt, Master Constable, Thomas Middleton, Thomas Dekker

Since Yesterday, Frederick Lewis Allen

The Scholemaster: Or, Plaine and Perfite Way of Teachyng Children the Latin Tong , Roger Ascham

The Wonderful Year, 1603, Thomas Dekker

Waverley, Sir Walter Scott

Guy Mannering, Sir Walter Scott

Old Mortality, Sir Walter Scott

The Knight of Malta, John Fletcher

Space Prison, Tom Godwin

The Home of the Blizzard Being the Story of the Australasian Antarctic Expedition, 1911-1914, Douglas Mawson

Wild-goose Chase , John Fletcher

If You Know Not Me, You Know Nobody. Part I and Part II, Thomas Heywood

The Ragged Trousered Philanthropists, Robert Tressell

The Greater Trumps, Charles Williams

The Island of Sheep, John Buchan

Eyes of the Woods, Joseph Altsheler

The Club of Queer Trades, G. K. Chesterton

The Financier, Theodore Dreiser

Something of Myself, Rudyard Kipling

Law of Freedom in a Platform, or True Magistracy Restored, Gerrard Winstanley

Damon and Pithias, Richard Edwards

Dido Queen of Carthage: And, The Massacre at Paris, Christopher Marlowe

Cocoa and Chocolate: Their History from Plantation to Consumer, Arthur Knapp

Lady of Pleasure, James Shirley

The South Pole: An account of the Norwegian Antarctic expedition in the "Fram," 1910-12. Volume 1 and Volume 2, Roald Amundsen

A Yorkshire Tragedy, Thomas Middleton (attrib.)

The Tragedy of Soliman and Perseda, Thomas Kyd

The Rape of Lucrece. Thomas Heywood

                                   and many others…

Tell us what you would love to see in print again, at affordable prices!
Email: **benedictionbooks@btinternet.com**